Praise for *Be a G[...]*
Solver - [...]

'Adrian Reed delivers comprehensive advice backed up by practical examples and relevant techniques. This is a well-organised book that provides an excellent toolkit for business problem-solvers.'

Debra Paul, Managing Director, AssistKD

'At last, a book that transforms a minefield of problem-solving theories into easily understood concepts that absolutely anyone can apply within both their work and personal lives. Compelling, relevant and, ultimately, essential reading.'

John Hackett, Managing Director and Organisational Change Alchemist, Franklin-Hackett Ltd

'A very enjoyable and pragmatic book for the most junior and senior executive who is often confronted with tricky daily problems and looking not just for a quick solution, but a strategy and approach to the solution.'

Stephen Ashworth, President and CEO, International Institute of Business Analysis (IIBA)

'Adrian offers a clear, step-by-step process, supported by proven techniques, visuals and hands-on tips to help you shift from solution building to problem solving. Inspiring for people new to the BA role, a solid reference for experienced ones.'

Filip Hendrickx, Business Consultant and Speaker bringing Lean Startup to established organisations, altershape

'If you are looking for a practical, structured way to solve any problem, this is your book. One of the best skills it teaches is how to make sure you are working on the right problem in the first place!'

Kupe Kupersmith, President, B2T Training

'An essential and highly accessible compendium of sensible and logical tools and techniques.'

Will Noble, Managing Director, Asia Pacific, Human Systems International (HSI)

Be a Great Problem Solver - Now!

PEARSON

At Pearson, we believe in learning – all kinds of learning for all kinds of people. Whether it's at home, in the classroom or in the workplace, learning is the key to improving our life chances.

That's why we're working with leading authors to bring you the latest thinking and best practices, so you can get better at the things that are important to you. You can learn on the page or on the move, and with content that's always crafted to help you understand quickly and apply what you've learned.

If you want to upgrade your personal skills or accelerate your career, become a more effective leader or more powerful communicator, discover new opportunities or simply find more inspiration, we can help you make progress in your work and life.

Pearson is the world's leading learning company. Our portfolio includes the Financial Times and our education business, Pearson International.

Every day our work helps learning flourish, and wherever learning flourishes, so do people.

To learn more, please visit us at www.pearson.com/uk

Be a Great Problem Solver - Now!

The 2-in-1 Manager: Speed Read - instant tips; Big Picture - lasting results

Adrian Reed

PEARSON

Harlow, England • London • New York • Boston • San Francisco • Toronto • Sydney
Auckland • Singapore • Hong Kong • Tokyo • Seoul • Taipei • New Delhi
Cape Town • São Paulo • Mexico City • Madrid • Amsterdam • Munich • Paris • Milan

Pearson Education Limited
Edinburgh Gate
Harlow CM20 2JE
United Kingdom
Tel: +44 (0)1279 623623
Web: www.pearson.com/uk

First edition published 2016 (print and electronic)

ISBN: 978-1-292-11962-5 (print)
        978-1-292-11965-6 (PDF)
        978-1-292-11964-9 (ePub)

British Library Cataloguing-in-Publication Data
A catalogue record for the print edition is available from the British Library

Library of Congress Cataloging-in-Publication Data
A catalog record for the print edition is available from the Library of Congress

10 9 8 7 6 5 4 3 2 1
20 19 18 17 16

Cover design by Two Associates

Print edition typeset in 10pt Scene Std by SPi Global
Printed in Great Britain by Henry Ling Ltd, at the Dorset Press, Dorchester, Dorset

NOTE THAT ANY PAGE CROSS REFERENCES REFER TO THE PRINT EDITION

To Larraine: For the advice you gave me on a cold, hostile, Rochester morning that I remember to this day.

To Dave: For leading by example and for creating memories that will never fade.

Contents

Contents

Contents

Contents

About the author

 **Adrian Reed** is an enthusiastic business analyst and consultant who loves working with others to solve tricky problems. He is Principal Consultant at Blackmetric Business Solutions, a niche business analysis training and consulting firm based in the UK. He speaks internationally on topics related to business analysis and problem solving, and enthusiastically believes in the benefits of good problem definition and business analysis.

For more information about Adrian's company, visit www. blackmetric.co.uk

You can read Adrian's blog at www.adrianreed.co.uk

Introduction

We live in a fast-moving world where problems, threats and opportunities must be assessed, prioritised and dealt with as quickly as possible. Yet problem solving is inherently complicated – rarely do problems exist in isolation. It is quite possible to solve a problem in *one* area and cause a brand new (potentially) worse problem somewhere else. It would be equally possible to solve a problem in a way that *we* think is fantastic – but that our stakeholders hate or that is out of alignment with our external business environment.

This is made all the more tricky by the fact that people often fall in *love* with potential solutions – before they have identified the problem they are actually trying to solve. Perhaps our boss comes in on a Monday morning and announces that we need to kick off a new project to purchase and implement a brand new IT system which will be the 'silver bullet' to solve all of our organisational ills. If we (and they) have not identified the problem or opportunity that they are trying to address, then we are likely to be heading for disappointment. Anyone who has wasted money on a shiny gadget (that looked great in the shop), only to find that it didn't change our lives can probably relate to this. We buy a 'solution' to the wrong problem!

This highlights that holistic problem-solving skills are crucial for any leader or manager. Yet it can be difficult to know where to start. In writing this book, I set out to bring together and discuss a practical set of tools and techniques that can be used to analyse problems in a consistent way. They certainly aren't the *only* tools available – but I have found them to be effective, useful and productive. More importantly, this book covers a *process* for problem solving, based around a one-page 'problem canvas'. You are completely free to use this canvas in your own organisations, and a downloadable copy is available at the book's website www.problemsolvingbook.co.uk. You'll find other useful links and resources there too.

This book is designed to be a practical reference guide, and one that you'll refer to time and time again. I hope you find it useful, enjoyable and that it helps in your problem-solving efforts.

All the best,

Adrian Reed

Principal Consultant,

Blackmetric Business Solutions

adrian.reed@problemsolvingbook.co.uk

Acknowledgements

We are grateful to the following for permission to reproduce copyright material:

Photos

Photo on p. 3 © BamboOK/Shutterstock; photo on p. 5 © Img Raj/Shutterstock; photo on p. 6 © 3Dstock/Shutterstock; photos on pp. 7, 25, 174 and 197 © Gunnar Pippel/Shutterstock; photos on pp. 8 and 76 © Sashkin/Shutterstock; photo on p. 9 © Mmaxer/Shutterstock; photo on p. 12 © PhotoSmile/Shutterstock; photo on p. 20 © Alina Ku-Ku/Shutterstock; photos on pp. 28 and 39 © Marekuliasz/Shutterstock; photos on pp. 40, 52, 172 and 201 © Michael D. Brown/Shutterstock; photos on p. 41 and 44 © VLADGRIN/Shutterstock; photo on p. 42 © Orla/Shutterstock; photo on p. 43 © SergeyDV/Shutterstock; photo on p. 45 © Vector-RGB/Shutterstock; photo on p. 48 © Rashevskyi Viacheslav/Shutterstock; photo on p. 57 © Tuulijumala/Shutterstock; photo on p. 60 © Marafona/Shutterstock; photo on p. 72 © Scrugglegreen/Shutterstock; photos on pp. 73 and 84 © Olivier Le Moal/Shutterstock; photo on p. 77 © A1Stock/Shutterstock; photo on p. 97 ©Jojje/Shutterstock; photo on p. 105 © Tan Kian Khoon/Shutterstock; photos on pp. 106 and 231 © Lord and Leverett/Pearson Education Ltd; photo on p. 108 © dadabosh/Shutterstock; photo on p. 109 © Mack2happy/Shutterstock; photo on p. 111 © Worker/Shutterstock; photo on p. 113 © 123rf.com; photo on p. 119 © Minerva Studio/Shutterstock; photo on p. 122 © David Lee/Shutterstock; photo on p. 130 © Mauro Saivezzo/Shutterstock; photos on pp. 137 and

145 © Lightspring/Shutterstock; photo on p. 138 © nasirkhan/ Shutterstock; photo on p. 141 © Dimec/Shutterstock; photo on p. 142 © Roobcio/Shutterstock; photo on p. 143 © Veerachai Viteeman/Shutterstock; photo on p. 148 © Palto/Shutterstock; photo on p. 158 © Sergii Korolko/Shutterstock; photos on pp. 160 and 218 © Nelson Marques/Shutterstock; photo on p. 162 © JohnKwan/Shutterstock; photo on p. 170 © Zphoto/Shutterstock; photos on pp. 171 and 186 © StockLite/Shutterstock; photo on p. 173 © ALMAGAMI/Shutterstock; photo on p. 175 © John Foxx Collection/Imagestate; photo on p. 184 © iQoncept/Shutterstock; photo on p. 190 © cybrain/Shutterstock; photo on p. 207 © rnl/ Shutterstock; photo on p. 208 © pedrosala/Shutterstock; photo on p. 209 © mypokcik/Shutterstock; photo on p. 210 © Andrey_ Kuzmin/Shutterstock; photo on p. 211 © Syda Productions/ Shutterstock; photo on p. 212 © push-to-grave/Shutterstock; photos on pp. 213 and 237 © Gines Valera Marin/Shutterstock; photo on p. 221 © volk6/Shutterstock.

Figures

Figures on pp. 4 and 16 © Assist Knowledge Development Ltd; figures on pp. 22 and 23 from *A Guide to the Business Analysis Body of Knowledge,* 3rd edn, © 2015 International Institute of Business Analysis. All rights reserved. Material produced with permission from IIBA; figures on pp. 18, 33, 34–5, 59, 169 and 180–1 © Blackmetric Business Solutions; figure on p. 55 adapted from Wilkins, A. and Archer, J., 'Creative Problem Solving – The Swiss Army Knife for BAs', a presentation at the BA conference Europe 2011; figure on p. 90 reprinted by permission of Harvard Business Review Press, from Kaplan, R. S. and Norton, D. P, *The Balanced Scorecard: Translating Strategy Into Action.* Copyright © 1995 by the Harvard Business Publishing Corporation, all rights reserved; symbols used in figure on p. 110 adapted from Podeswa, H., *The Business Analyst's Handbook,* 1e © 2009 Delmar Learning, a part of Cengage Learning, Inc. Reproduced by permission, www. cengage.com/permissions

Chapter 1

Avoid the solution trap

1.1 What's wrong with a knee-jerk solution?

In a fast-moving business environment, we are often under significant pressure to solve business problems quickly. Yet a trap awaits the unprepared. So many businesses make knee-jerk decisions that *compound* rather than *solve* their problems. Newspapers are littered with stories of business initiatives that have failed, and organisations that have lost money and even their competitive edge by pursuing ill-advised decisions or solutions. These failures can occur for many complex reasons, but one common cause is that organisations make an early decision on what route to take without carrying out sufficient analysis. We can avoid this trap by making sure we address the root cause of the problem (rather than just the symptoms or effects), and by keeping a constant guard against selecting a solution too soon.

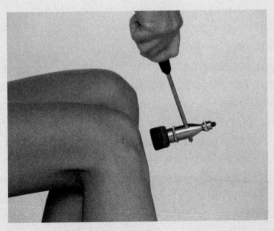

Source: BambOK/Shutterstock

Do this

Ask whether you are being presented with a pre-supposed solution, rather than the root problem. Ensure the right people have been involved with defining the problem, and use the techniques in this book to delve further to understand the root cause and to discover possible solutions.

1.2 Think holistically

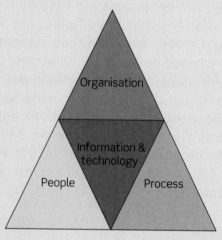

Source: Assist Knowledge Development Ltd

Organisations can be complex environments, and by solving a problem in one area we may inadvertently cause a problem elsewhere. For instance, solving a problem that enables more sales to be made is only useful if the production and dispatch departments have capacity to fulfil those orders! Successful problem solving relies on holistic thinking and the ability to think beyond the immediate problem area. Using the 'four-view' model of the business (people, process, organisation and technology) can help. It is likely that a change in any one of these areas may have knock-on impacts on the others – a new IT system may require training (people) and may alter the way the work is carried out (process). Thinking across teams and departments is also crucial.

Do this

Consider problems (and potential solutions) from multiple angles, including how they involve or will impact *people, processes, the organisation* and *IT*.

1.3 Structure your problem-solving approach

There is value in taking a structured approach to problem solving. It isn't necessary to use a complex or laborious problem-solving process, but it is very useful to consider a problem from three angles:

- **Why:** Why is the problem important? Why does it need to be solved *now*?
- **What:** What needs to change? What are the core requirements? What is the scope and scale of the problem-solving initiative?
- **How:** How could the problem be solved? How many options are available?

A range of techniques are available that help us understand more about the problem, these are described in more detail throughout this book.

Source: ImgRaj/Shutterstock

Do this

Step back and take a calculated approach to problem solving. Taking time to plan the approach will save time in the long run.

1.4 Scour the stakeholder landscape

Problems don't exist in a vacuum, and it's important that we understand who else is *interested* or *impacted by* the problem that we are examining. In large organisations, problems may have many stakeholders, and it's important that we plan our stakeholder engagement strategy. When it comes to stakeholder management, think ICE: identify, categorise and engage.

We start by *identifying* the likely stakeholders, and putting together a list. It is worth considering the relative levels of influence they hold, as well as how impacted they are by the problem. Also consider their *attitude*. Are they supportive, neutral, or might they actively object to any problem-solving activity? This allows us to *categorise* the stakeholders, perhaps using a traditional stakeholder grid (as explained in the 'Big picture' section). Once they are categorised we can plan how and when to *engage* them.

Source: 3Dstock/Shutterstock

Do this

Cast the net wide to ensure you have found and engaged the relevant stakeholders. Ensure stakeholders are *identified*, *categorised* and *engaged*.

1.5 Slow down to speed up: be prepared for challenge

Whilst there is clear benefit in taking a structured approach to decision making, it is likely that we'll come under pressure from our business stakeholders to hit the ground running. There can sometimes be a reluctance to spend time on problem analysis activities, as it may be seen as 'abstract' and wasteful. Whilst this type of feedback from our stakeholders could be seen as problematic, we can use it to our advantage. It shows that they are engaged, and are keen to see the problem solved. By showing them the benefit of the problem-solving approach, we can ensure that they are fully on board. We can explain that it won't waste time – and in fact, it may *save* time in the long run. Whilst we may be slowing down temporarily, this is so that we can hit the accelerator with confidence once we've found the best solution option.

Source: Gunnar Pippel/Shutterstock

Do this

Consider how you will handle resistance or challenge to a structured problem-solving approach. Consider using a problem canvas (discussed in Section 1.7 and Chapter 6) to illustrate the stages of a problem-solving process.

1.6 Uncover constraints

As we uncover more about a problem, we'll want to start thinking about ways to solve it. Yet, it is highly likely that there will be some factors that constrain the solutions that can be considered. It is likely that we'll have limited time, money and resources – and suggesting a solution that is in the wrong ballpark will crush our credibility. It's important that we surface constraints early, so we can make consistently credible recommendations. Constraints could include factors such as:

- Time
- Cost/resources
- Quality
- Scope
- Technology
- Business process
- Organisational structure
- Legislation/regulation

Source: Sashkin/Shutterstock

Do this

Understand what genuinely cannot shift or budge. Ensure that any proposed solutions fit within these boundaries.

1.7 Be concise yet precise: introducing the one-page problem canvas

Distilling a problem definition down onto a single sheet can help ensure that everyone involved is 'on the same page' and has a consistent and coherent view on the problem we are trying to solve. The problem canvas is one way of achieving this and provides a template where the problem statement, the scope and the likely solutions can be displayed and validated. The template (shown in the 'Big picture' section) is designed to show *just enough* information about the problem, and it is also a useful prompt or 'aide-memoire', helping us to ensure we have considered the relevant angles. A soft copy of the template can be downloaded from www.problemsolvingbook.co.uk

Source: Mmaxer/Shutterstock

Do this

Use the problem canvas template to develop a succinct definition of the problem, desired outcomes and to provide a list of possible solution options. Build this document iteratively and share it with your team and your stakeholders.

1.1 What's wrong with a knee-jerk solution?

Why

Many of us have probably worked with a co-worker or manager who has asked us to focus on *delivering a solution* rather than *analysing the problem*. In many ways, this is completely understandable – after all, in a fast-paced business environment, being able to solve problems *quickly* is essential. It might mean that we clinch an important deal or we usurp our competitors. Yet, counterintuitively, if we move *before* we have an adequate understanding of the problem we are trying to solve, we might fall into a trap and face serious consequences. We might end up recommending, implementing or buying a solution that just isn't right for our business – we might implement the wrong solution for our problem. Or even worse, we might find that different colleagues and stakeholders had a different interpretation on precisely which problem we are trying to solve – leading to conflict, delays and further expense. All situations that are best avoided!

The situations above describe knee-jerk reactions to problems. So often, problems are far more complex than they appear and the first solution that we imagine might not be the best one. Here are just a few examples:

- **Effect rather than cause:** Imagine that you are asked to look at streamlining your company's complaints-handling process, as your organisation can't respond to complaints quickly enough. Whilst this would undoubtedly be possible, it would be far more beneficial to understand *why* people are complaining, and address the root causes (so that they don't need to complain in the first place!).

- **A solution looking for a problem:** So often, we unconsciously *fall in love* with a particular idea or solution, so much so that we doggedly pursue it, even if it isn't fit for our needs. Anyone who has ever bought a shiny gadget, only for it to fall very quickly into disuse will have felt this pain. With a £30 smoothie-maker, this is inconvenient enough. When a business spends millions on an IT system that doesn't meet its needs, the effects can be crippling.

- **We're not on the same page:** Perhaps different people in the organisation have a subtly different interpretation of the problem we're trying to solve. Different people might have different motivations too, and without a careful appreciation of this we might end up disappointing some or all of our stakeholders!

Source: PhotoSmile/Shutterstock

Knowledge briefing

Lack of problem analysis can lead to significant wasted expenditure. To quote just one example: In around 2004, the UK government kicked off a project which aimed at making significant changes to the infrastructure used to handle emergency calls made to the fire and rescue service. The project aimed at providing more resilience and efficiencies, and focussed on consolidating the number of call centres required to handle the calls. As the project progressed, significant problems emerged – and then in 2010 the project was scrapped. Government reports show that the *minimum* amount of money wasted was £469 million, and to make things worse it appears not a *single* objective was achieved. It has been suggested that the *solution* that was being delivered was significantly over-specified and not appropriate to the actual needs of the country. Or, to put this differently, it may have been aiming to solve the wrong problem. It is a complex case, with many contributing factors, but it certainly appears that there were cheaper and more appropriate options available.

This is not a unique example. A government report went on to state:

> 'The issues leading up to this failed project are by no means unique or isolated. Government IT projects can appear to take on a life of their own, continuing to absorb resources without ever reaching their objectives.'
>
> (National Audit Office, 2011)

Whilst this example is taken from the public sector, there are similar failings in the private and third sectors too – although they are not always as visible. Failures of this type can affect all types of decision – from day-to-day operational decision making, right through to multi-million procurement decisions. Spending time up front to ensure that we're solving the right problem, when paired with good project management and business analysis, can help us to avoid these types of extensive failures.

How

Next time you are presented with a problem, override your subconscious mind's desire to jump on the first available solution and encourage those around you to take a step back. Rather than pursuing a knee-jerk reaction, use the techniques outlined in this book to ensure that everyone is on the same page and to search and evaluate a range of solutions. Ask yourself questions including:

1. Am I being presented with a solution, rather than a problem?

2. Have the right people been involved to define this problem?

3. Is this the root cause, or do we need to delve further?

4. Does this problem *really* have to be solved right now, or do we have time to consider options?

Utilise the techniques described throughout this book to delve further.

Reflection

- How did it work?

- What will I do next time?

References

National Audit Office, 2011. *The Failure of the FiReControl Project.* London: NAO.

1.2 Think holistically

Why

> '**Holistic:** *Characterised by the belief that the parts of something are intimately interconnected and explicable only by reference to the whole.*'
>
> (Oxford Dictionaries, n.d.)

To drive the best outcome when problem solving, it's important that we consider the problem situation *holistically*. Problems are often complex and messy, with many interconnected parts. What is presented to us as, say, a technology-related problem might actually be much wider ranging.

So often even a small incremental change to one part of a business can have much broader knock-on effects. By solving *our* localised problem, we might cause significant problems elsewhere.

Imagine a sales team that are desperately trying to drive up their sales volumes. They stock a brand new product, and the market *loves* it. They take hundreds of orders – and the sales revenues sky rocket. This sounds like good news – but if the procurement team couldn't *buy* the stock quickly enough, or if the dispatch process couldn't handle the volumes, then we'd be setting ourselves up to fail! Success in one area is fruitless if a problem is transferred elsewhere, and it's important that we consider the wider landscape (which may span teams, divisions or even organisations).

Knowledge briefing

In the seminal book *Business Analysis* (Paul, Cadle and Yeates, 2014), Debra Paul refers to a four-view model of a business, and encourages us to consider problem situations from the angles of *people, process, organisation* and *information technology*. It is very useful to consider this model when assessing a problem situation. It's also important to consider that a change in any one of the four areas is likely to impact the others.

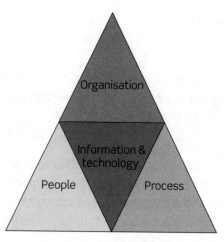

Source: Assist Knowledge Development Ltd

How

For example, automating a process may involve additional IT, re-training (people) and may even involve organisational structure changes (organisation). The four-view model can help us take a holistic approach by considering:

1. **People:** How are people rewarded, appraised and motivated? Could the targets they are set be contributing to the problem? What other metrics might be more appropriate? Is everyone adequately trained and up-to-speed on any relevant systems?

2. **Organisation:** Does the organisational structure help or hinder? Are there structural issues that contribute to the problem?

3. **Process:** How are the underlying business processes affected, impacted or involved in this problem? Are there process improvement opportunities? Where are the 'bottlenecks' and constraints? Who is involved in the process?

4. **Information and technology:** How is information technology currently used? What sort of systems are used, and are there any disconnects? Is there an opportunity for improvement? Are the existing systems used appropriately – or could they be used in additional or different ways?

Reflection

- How did it work?

> [blank response box]

- What will I do next time?

> [blank response box]

References

Oxford Dictionaries, n.d. *Oxford English Dictionary*. [Online] Available at: http://www.oxforddictionaries.com/definition/english/holistic

POPIT™ Model, from Paul, D., Cadle, J. and Yeates, D. (eds), 2014. *Business Analysis*. Third Edition. Swindon: BCS. Copyright and trademark of Assist KD Ltd.

1.3 Structure your problem-solving approach

Why

When the heat is on, and when a problem is seemingly urgent, it can be very comforting and natural to reach out for the first available solution – without considering the problem any further. In some circumstances, this might be the best approach – if you're on a sinking ship then you probably haven't got much time to evaluate your options and making a quick and decisive decision may save you. However, often urgency is an *illusion* – and by structuring our problem-solving approach we can break through this illusion and ensure that we achieve the best possible outcome.

Knowledge briefing

A problem-solving process provides us with a repeatable method of considering and analysing the problem situation. It forms the backbone of our problem analysis activities – of course, we can expand and embellish it where necessary, but it provides us with a re-usable framework. Bedding in and establishing a framework ensures that everyone involved has a common understanding of what will take place, and what will happen next at each stage. Importantly, taking a structured approach to problem solving can ensure that we take a step back, and help us and our stakeholders avoid falling for a knee-jerk solution.

How

We don't need a complicated or laborious process, in fact it can be useful to structure problem-solving activities around three important questions:

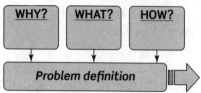

Source: Blackmetric Business Solutions

1. **Why:** It is important that we understand *why* there needs to be a change to the status quo. If a problem exists, *why* does it need to be solved? Why is it so urgent, and why does it demand our attention now? Why is there even a problem in the first place – has the root cause really been identified?

2. **What:** It's also important that we understand the scope and scale of the problem; or to put it another way, it's important that we know *what* needs to change. Referring back to the four-view model mentioned in the previous section, which processes, people, IT systems or organisational structures are we changing? Which others might be impacted?

3. **How:** Alongside understanding *why* and *what,* it is also important that we understand *how* the problem can be solved. This involves imagining and evaluating solution options, and may involve presenting a recommendation to our stakeholders. Perhaps a process change will help solve the problem, or a new IT application, or a combination of changes.

Chapters 2–7 cover some really practical techniques for understanding and documenting the why, the what and the how.

Reflection

- How did it work?

- What will I do next time?

1.4 Scour the stakeholder landscape

Why

It is likely that different stakeholders in our organisation will have different perspectives on a problem – and some may see the problem very differently to others. In order to really understand a problem, it's crucial that we understand and consider these perspectives. Before we can understand these perspectives, we need to scour the landscape and identify the relevant stakeholders.

Source: Alina Ku-Ku/Shutterstock

Knowledge briefing

It is worth taking a step back and reflecting on what we mean by *stakeholder*. A stakeholder can be defined as:

> '*A group or individual with a relationship to the change, the need or the solution.*'
>
> (Business Analysis Body of Knowledge (BABOK) guide v3)

In essence, a stakeholder is anyone with an *interest* in the problem we are trying to solve or the solution we are trying to create. They might be internal or external to our organisation, and they may or may not support our problem-solving efforts. It is crucial that we identify them.

How

It is worth considering the wider stakeholder landscape and to look beyond the obvious subjects. Ask questions including:

1. Who might be involved or impacted?

2. Who might have authority or power over the situation?

3. Is each stakeholder supportive of the problem-solving work, or are they likely to be actively resistant?

Spreading the net wide can pay dividends, considering not just internal but external stakeholders too. There are three key steps to stakeholder management, summarised by the acronym ICE: identify, categorise, engage.

Identify

It can be useful to compile a list of stakeholders, noting down their role and the type of interest that they have in the problem situation. It is worth thinking about the relative *influence level* they have, on a scale of 0–10. It is also worth considering how much the problem (or the potential solution) impacts them, again on a relative scale of 0–10. An example is shown below:

Name	Role	Interest	Influence level (0–10)	Impacted level (0–10)
John Smith	Operations Manager	His team is directly affected by the problem. Keen supporter	10	10
Jayne Brown	Compliance Manager	Needs to ensure we deliver a legal and compliant solution	8	2
etc . . .				

This list is an important first step, and can help us to plan and prepare for which stakeholders we'll need to liaise with.

Categorise

Having identified and noted down our stakeholders in the way described above, a further logical step is to *categorise* them. There will be some stakeholders who we need to pay more active attention to, and some who are more involved, interested or hold more power over the problem situation. It can be useful to map our stakeholders onto a traditional stakeholder matrix, such as the one shown below. This can help us identify stakeholders that have similar characteristics:

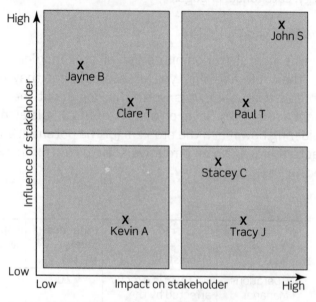

Source: Adapted from *A Guide to the Business Analysis Body of Knowledge*, 3rd edn, International Institute of Business Analysis (IIBA, 2015)

Knowing where each stakeholder sits on the grid can help us define communication, engagement and stakeholder management strategies, as illustrated in the diagram below.

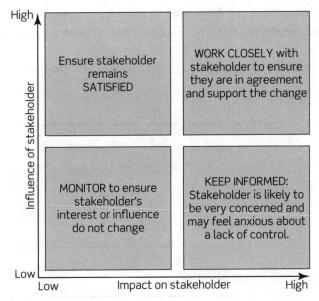

Source: *A Guide to the Business Analysis Body of Knowledge*, 3rd edn, International Institute of Business Analysis (IIBA, 2015)

Engage

Having identified and categorised our stakeholders, it is important to consider how to engage them.

The stakeholder matrix above gives a useful summary of which stakeholders we'll be needing to actively engage with. Other questions to consider include:

- Who has a view or opinion on the problem?
- Which stakeholders need convincing?
- Who do we need to meet or interview, and when?
- How often do we need to liaise with each stakeholder?
- What insight or information do they hold?
- How would they like to receive information from us?
- What would their role in any problem-solving initiative be?

A thorough understanding of the relevant stakeholders' perspectives and points of view can help us ensure that we succeed in our problem solving and deliver the required business outcome. Putting together a plan to engage the relevant stakeholders, based on the matrix above, can be a significant help.

Reflection

- How did it work?

- What will I do next time?

References

International Institute of Business Analysis (IIBA), 2015. *A Guide to the Business Analysis Body of Knowledge® (Guide®)*, v3. Toronto: IIBA.

1.5 Slow down to speed up: be prepared for challenge

Why

'In the pressure to get things done, many managers fear being patient. They focus on short-term fixes to existing problems rather than on instituting processes to solve and eventually prevent problems and to identify unsuspected opportunities.

But as in the fable of the tortoise and the hare, the companies that seem to move most slowly and laboriously at the start often lead their industries by the end of the day.'

(Sirkin and Stalk, 1990)

In organisations of all types, it is likely that there will be resistance to taking time out to really think a problem through. So often, there is (quite rightly) a sense of urgency – a feeling that we just *have* to start moving quickly. This can lead to the temptation to solve our problem by implementing the first solution that we come across, and this can result in the significant and wasteful types of problems that were discussed in Section 1.1.

It's important to be prepared for – and welcome – this type of challenge. Although it may appear problematic, resistance of this type shows that our stakeholders are engaged and want to make a difference. It can provide a useful opportunity for us to gain feedback and validate our assumptions. At the same time, it is crucial that we subtly nudge our stakeholders towards a holistic problem-solving approach, and encourage a calculated approach to problem solving.

Source: Gunnar Pippel/Shutterstock

Knowledge briefing

A study of 343 businesses (carried out by The Forum Corporation, reported in *Harvard Business Review* in 2010) found that companies that reacted quickly but *didn't* take time to periodically reflect and ensure they were on the right track ended up with lower sales and operating profits. Those that paused at key moments averaged 40 per cent higher sales and 52 per cent higher operating profits over a three-year period (Davis and Atkinson, 2010).

How

1. When embarking on problem-solving activities, think about *how* you'll overcome resistance. How will you 'sell' the problem-solving process, and which stakeholders will you most likely need to sell it to?

2. Consider whether you might want to use an example problem canvas (discussed in Section 1.7 and Chapter 6) to illustrate the stages of a problem-solving process to your stakeholders. Consider how you'll sell the benefits of thinking holistically.

3. Use the 'four-view model' of the business mentioned in Section 1.2 to showcase the importance of holistic thinking.

4. Share examples of problem-solving successes from within your organisation – as well as high-profile external failures from outside – to show the benefits that a robust yet streamlined process can bring. Remember that slowing down early can mean that we accelerate with confidence once a solution has been chosen.

Reflection

- How did it work?

- What will I do next time?

[ ]

References

Davis, J.R. and Atkinson, T., 2010. 'Need speed? Slow down', *Harvard Business Review*, May.

Sirkin, H.L. and Stalk, G., 1990. 'Fix the process, not the problem', *Harvard Business Review*, July–August.

1.6 Uncover constraints

Why

When we are looking for ways of solving a problem, it is unlikely that we'll have unlimited time, money and resources. We'll need to solve the problem within certain boundaries and within certain *constraints*.

A constraint can be defined as:

> *'An influencing factor that cannot be changed, and that places a limit or restriction on a possible solution or solution option.'*
> (International Institute of Business Analysis (IIBA), 2015)

As implied by the definition, constraints can be wide ranging. We might be constrained by factors including:

- **Time:** We may be under pressure to deliver a solution within a particular timeframe. If we worked in a busy retail outlet preparing for the Christmas rush, solving a problem with the Christmas display after the festive season would be largely pointless!

- **Cost/resources:** It is very likely that we'll have limited resources, and it's important that we consider which solutions are achievable given any resource constraints.

- **Quality:** In some cases, quality can't be compromised. If your problem relates to a life-or-death situation, quality may be the most important factor.

- **Scope:** Certain elements may be outside (or inside) of our remit.

- **Technology:** We may have specific technical constraints – perhaps we can't change particular IT systems, or perhaps any solution *must* fit with our existing systems.

- **Business process:** It may be necessary for any solution we implement to fit in with an existing set of business processes.

- **Organisational structure:** The organisational structure may be constrained.

- **Legislation/regulation:** Our organisation may be compelled to carry out its business in a certain way, and this may impact our ability to solve problems.

Source: Marekuliasz/Shutterstock

Knowledge briefing

Knowing any constraints we are under is essential – this prevents us from spending time investigating solutions that would never be appropriate. However, when we uncover a constraint it is equally important for us to feel empowered to validate that it *really is* immovable. In some cases there may be perceived rules and limitations that can be challenged and may be subject to change.

Constraints are often perceived as negative, but providing they are clearly signposted from the outset, they can help drive innovation. As the saying goes 'Necessity is the mother of invention', and having constrained resources may lead us to considering new and innovative solutions that we wouldn't have otherwise uncovered. Either way, it is crucial that we are aware of them.

Constraints can be captured and communicated using a simple constraint log. This can be as simple or elaborate as you need it to be, but as a minimum it is valuable to capture the following information about each constraint:

ID	Constraint	Rationale	Owner	Last updated	Due for review
C01	The solution must be delivered within a budget of £10,000	A fixed budget has been agreed; there will be insufficient financial benefits to warrant exceeding this budget	Steven D	6th Dec	6th Mar
C02	Any technological element must interface with an IAL SD/500 Series server	Our core customer database is stored on an IAL SD/500 Series, and a strategic architectural decision has been made to ensure all components interface or are compatible with this	Jayne B	2nd Nov	2nd Feb

The constraint log can be expanded with additional columns as needed, for example to include categories, priorities, impact levels and so on. However, the important first step is to identify and capture each constraint.

How

1. Understand the business environment that your organisation works in. What legislation and regulations are relevant and prominent?

2. Ask key stakeholders what is most important: cost, time or quality?

3. Understand what is *driving* the need to solve the problem. Why is this problem important *now*?

4. Gauge the appetite for change. Are stakeholders expecting an incremental, small change to solve the problem? Or are they anticipating a larger scale change?

5. Ask the questions outright: 'What are our constraints?' and 'What is immovable?'

6. Understand the culture of the organisation. What is considered 'beyond the pale'? Can this be creatively nudged or challenged, or is it a hard constraint?

7. Capture and log the constraints so that they can be kept 'front of mind' throughout the project-solving initiative. As a minimum capture a description of the constraint, its owner, and the date that it should be revisited or checked. It is also good practice to assign a reference to each constraint so it can be cross-referenced.

8. Ensure each constraint is captured precisely and unambiguously so there is no room for doubt.

Reflection

• How did it work?

- What will I do next time?

References

International Institute of Business Analysis (IIBA), 2015. *A Guide to the Business Analysis Body of Knowledge® (Guide®)*, v3. Toronto: IIBA.

1.7 Be concise yet precise: introducing the one-page problem canvas

Why

As alluded to in the previous sections of this chapter, for our problem-solving activities to be successful, it's *essential* that we are all on the 'same page'. It's crucial that we and our stakeholders have a common view of the nature and scope of the problem that we're trying to solve. It's also important that we highlight any constraints – things that can't be changed – so that we come up with solution options that are feasible and implementable.

It is very easy and tempting to dive into the detail early, and start examining granular data about the perceived problem and any likely solutions. However, this can lead to 'analysis paralysis' – a pattern where we delve into too much detail too early, leading to it becoming practically impossible to make a decision. Before we expend too much effort, it is very valuable to validate that we all have a common view of the context of the problem.

A very useful way of doing this is to summarise the problem onto a one-page 'problem canvas'. This canvas is a concise yet precise way of defining the problem scope as well as documenting likely solutions. An example of a problem canvas is included below, and the canvas is explained in detail in Chapter 6. You can download a free version of the canvas template by visiting www. problemsolvingbook.co.uk

Knowledge briefing

Even the most complex of situations can normally be distilled down to a single page, and the activity of doing so helps us crystallise and focus on the most important elements. Having a structured template or canvas helps us to avoid missing any crucial aspects. Toyota famously advocated use of visual management and the use of single-page A3-sized reports.

> 'The A3 reports are often posted on visual display boards; they are standardized and designed to follow a pattern that can be understood and digested at a glance. It is hard to imagine a problem-solving exercise that does not involve creating diagrams and charts of a system or process to help people clarify their thinking and make sure that nothing has been missed.'

> (Liker and Convis, 2012)

When utilising a single-page report or canvas, it is crucial to focus on the *quality* and *relevance* of the information that we choose to display. It's important that we see this document as a crucial communication aid – not just a 'tick box' step in a problem-solving process. We should focus on being both concise yet also precise – our aim is to quickly and unambiguously communicate the problem and potential solution options.

Each section of the problem canvas is elaborated and explained further in the following chapters of this book. The key sections on the canvas link directly to the three questions mentioned in Section 1.3:

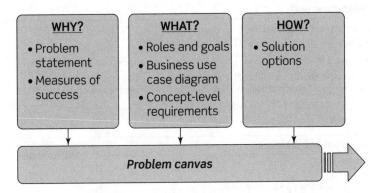

Source: Blackmetric Business Solutions

A quick reference guide to the main sections on the canvas is shown below:

Problem-solving question	Problem canvas section	Summary	Described in Section
Why?	Problem/ opportunity description	A concise and precise statement of the problem (or opportunity) being solved	2.2
	Measures of success	Critical success factors (CSFs) and key performance indicators (KPIs) that help us track success	3.2–3.4
What?	Indicative scope	Using the 'roles and goals' technique and/or drawing a business use case diagram to indicate scope of the problem	4.3–4.5
How?	Potential solution options identified	A list of potential solutions for consideration	5.1–5.7

Avoid the solution trap

Example: problem canvas

Problem name	**Busy phone lines**	Canvas ID	1203-17
Canvas author	Simon Bannatyne	Canvas version	1.0

Problem/Opportunity description

The problem of congested and busy phone lines

Affects our customers and call centre staff

The impact of which is we lose potential sales... as customers can't get through

A successful solution would enable customers to get information and make a purchase quickly without being on hold, leading to increased revenues (and profits)

Concept-level requirements

Summary:

Enable customers to quickly and efficiently:

- Place orders
- Make enquiries about existing orders

Indicative scope

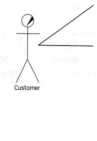

Customer

Potential solution options identified:

Option	Comment
Re-vamp website Accept orders online	Would also lower transaction costs
Install smart-call routing	Would ensure customers get to the right person first time
Re-vamp website Provide better information (but no transactions) online	Lower cost option Enables customers to find answers to simple queries online
Install more phone lines and employ more agents	Scale up operations

Source: Blackmetric Business Solutions

Portfolio	XYZ Portfolio	Sponsor	Lynda Jones	Confidence:	**Green**
Date	1 January	Status	Submitted for review		

Benefits/Measures of success

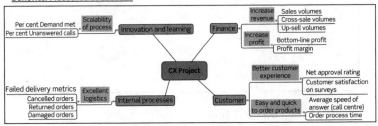

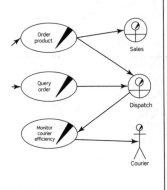

Attach further information/appendices here

Including confidence rationale, additional requirements, artefacts etc

Attach CARID log here

(Constraints, assumptions, risks, issues, dependencies)

Recommended next steps

1. Carry out a feasibility study to establish which potential solution is most appropriate
2. Gather high level business requirements
3. Put together an outline business case to establish quantifiable benefits

Resources required

Estimated completion date: 1 November

1 BA required

Reflection

- How did it work?

[blank response box]

- What will I do next time?

[blank response box]

References

Liker, J.K and Convis, G.L., 2012. *The Toyota Way to Lean Leadership*, New York: McGraw-Hill.

Chapt

Think problem *before* solution

2.1 The importance of 'why'

When problem solving it is important to thoroughly assess and understand the current situation, and avoid jumping to a conclusion over what the right solution might be. Problem solving works best when we generate different solution options. With multiple possibilities on the table we can carry out an evaluation to compare and contrast each option and conclude which will be the most important.

This starts with a thorough understanding of *why* the problem is a problem in the first place. It is useful to consider:

- *Why* the problem is occurring
- *Why* it is worth solving.

These themes are discussed throughout Chapter 2.

Source: Marekuliasz/Shutterstock

Do this

When embarking on problem solving, spend time assessing why the problem is important, and what the root causes are. The 'five whys' technique is invaluable as it allows us to probe and understand a particular stakeholder's perspective on what causes a problem, and it can also help us uncover the reasons why solving a problem is considered valuable.

2.2 Defining a problem or opportunity statement

An important first step to solving a problem is to *define it.* Stakeholders often have subtly (or vastly) different interpretations of the problem that is being considered, and the scope of the problem-solving exercise. Left unchecked, this could lead to conflict and a mismatch of expectations – we may inadvertently solve the problem in a way that meets the needs of only some of our stakeholders. Or, even worse, we may inadvertently make things *worse* for one group of stakeholders.

A problem (or an opportunity) can be defined with a concise and precise problem or opportunity statement. Working with stakeholders to create this will ensure that everyone is 'on the same page' and there is a clear view on the nature and scope of the problem that is being examined and solved. The problem will help manage expectations and keep the problem-solving initiative on the right track and within an agreed scope.

Source: Michael D. Brown/Shutterstock

Do this

Work with stakeholders to create a succinct and agreed problem or opportunity statement. Ensure that there is agreement over the wording. A useful problem statement format, provided by IIBA's *A Guide to the Business Analysis Body of Knowledge® (Guide®)* v2.0 is:

The problem of . . . Affects . . . The impact of which is . . . A successful solution would . . .

2.3 Encourage divergent and convergent thinking

It can be useful to consider different ways of thinking when problem solving. Two contrasting but complementary ways are *divergent* and *convergent* thinking.

When we are initially brainstorming, perhaps to uncover potential contributing factors that affect the problem (or when initially creating a 'long list' of potential solution options), it is useful to encourage *divergent thinking*. We want to encourage a variety of ideas, without (yet) evaluating whether they are viable or effective. We are encouraging quantity over quality.

However, at later stages of the problem-solving process we will be encouraging *convergent* thinking – taking long lists of potential contributing factors (or potential solutions) and narrowing them down to those that are relevant.

Source: VLADGRIN/Shutterstock

Do this

Throughout the problem-solving process, consider whether convergent or divergent thinking would be most useful/ appropriate. Ensure that creative thinking/brainstorming exercises are designed to encourage these types of thinking – and remember that it is possible to switch between them in a single session, providing the attendees are suitably briefed.

2.4 Get to the root of the problem

When we are initially presented with a problem, it is possible that we will be observing the *symptoms.* We might observe a drop in profits, or a rise in customer complaints. Whilst it is important to understand the nature and severity of the symptoms, it is crucial to assess and understand the *root cause.* Treating the symptoms may provide temporary relief, but addressing the root cause will prevent the problem from recurring in future.

As previously mentioned, the 'five whys' technique can be an extremely useful starting point. Alongside this, it is useful to use a fishbone diagram to consider and catalogue the various underlying and contributing factors to the problem.

Source: Orla/Shutterstock

Do this

Work with your team and any other interested stakeholders to create a fishbone diagram. Think broadly about factors that contribute to the problem. Evolve and iterate the diagram as the problem-solving initiative continues and as a richer understanding of the problem is attained.

2.5 Consider the external environment

Organisations don't exist within a self-contained bubble, they are influenced and impacted by factors that are outside of their boundaries and outside of their control. Like the crew aboard a ship assessing the proposed route and considering the weather and tide, it is important that we understand the changing influences that are in our external environments. These influences include political, economic, social-cultural trends and so on. In many cases these factors may *constrain* the problem-solving options available to us – for example: legislation or regulation may prevent us from solving a problem in a certain way, or changing social trends may mean that some solutions are more 'on trend' than others.

It is therefore important that we analyse and assess the external business environment when embarking on a problem-solving initiative. This will help in preventing us from delivering a solution that *we* think is perfect but that is ultimately rejected as it is out of line with the *business environment*.

Source: SergeyDV/Shutterstock

Do this

Use external business environmental analysis techniques such as STEEPLE to analyse and consider the wider picture.

2.6 Consider multiple perspectives on the problem

As outlined in Section 2.1, it is likely that there will be a number of stakeholders who have an interest in (or who are impacted by) the problem being considered. They may have very different perspectives on the problem that we are trying to solve. It is important that we take their views into account so that we (ideally) create a solution that works for all parties. It is equally important as these stakeholders may hold the key to us thoroughly understanding the problem and any potential solutions.

By involving and engaging a broad range of stakeholders we are aiming for a complete and coherent view of the problem situation, whilst gaining commitment from those that will need to be involved or who will be affected.

Source: VLADGRIN/Shutterstock

Do this
Ask questions like 'Who else might be affected by this problem?' or 'Who might be interested in a solution to this problem?' Take time to understand differing perspectives, and where conflict occurs, bring people together to discuss.

2.7 Gain consensus and move forward

Bringing stakeholders together is useful, but ultimately it is important that we gain consensus and the commitment to move forward. The diagrams and artefacts that we have discussed previously (including the problem statement and fishbone diagram) can be used to create a conversation. They can be iteratively built and incrementally tweaked as more information becomes available – and they are extremely useful when seeking to validate that a common view of the problem exists.

Bringing people together in a problem validation workshop can be extremely effective. Any differences of opinion can be discussed and hopefully resolved. The fishbone diagram and problem statement can be annotated and updated to create versions that everyone agrees to and buys into.

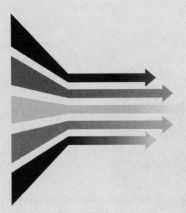

Source: Vector-RGB/Shutterstock

Do this

Bring people together to ensure there is a common understanding of the problem. Use the problem statement and fishbone diagram to drive a conversation. Consider annotating the fishbone diagram with a scope boundary indicating which root causes/contributing factors are within the scope of the problem-solving exercise (and which are not).

out catalogues to customers who subsequently place an order via phone. The company has started to receive a large number of complaints from its customers – in fact, it is now receiving complaints faster than it can respond. There is a desire to implement a new complaints handling procedure, to ensure that complaints can be resolved quickly – but we feel that this is somewhat of a knee-jerk reaction. Perhaps we feel that rather than addressing the complaints handling process, it would be better to understand the root causes of the complaints themselves and address them! So we decide to utilise the 'five whys' technique to find out more. Our conversation might go something like this:

Q1: Can you tell me why you're keen on implementing a new complaints handling process?

A1: Yes, of course. We've seen a massive increase in the number of complaints in the last 12 months, this has led to more complaints than we can handle.

Q2: Why has the level of complaints increased?

A2: There's a number of reasons – but one significant factor is that we've started to take on more customers generally.

Q3: Why is taking on additional customers a problem?

A3: More customers is a positive thing, of course! The problem is that orders from our customers tend to arrive in peaks and troughs, often in response to special offers and marketing campaigns. When there's a peak, we simply can't shift their orders out of the door quickly enough.

Q4: Why is it that you can't shift the orders quickly enough?

A4: Because we don't have enough staff on.

Q5: Can you tell me why there aren't always enough staff scheduled to work?

A5: It really goes back to what I was saying earlier – our staffing level is static, and a year ago a ban on overtime was brought in.

Due to the peaks and troughs in demand we are often unable to meet demand.

Of course, we could keep going, but in just five questions we've gained a much more thorough understanding of the problem. In fact, rather than simply improving the complaints handling process, in this example it would almost certainly be more valuable to work on predicting and managing demand so that there weren't complaints in the first place!

How

1. Recognise when a solution is being proposed without a full understanding of the problem.

2. Encourage the team to take a step back and examine the problem situation before proceeding head-first into a solution. Encourage a focus on the root causes.

3. Use 'five whys' to develop a better understanding of the problem and its root causes.

4. Utilise the other problem-analysis techniques in this section to develop a well-rounded view of the problem, and the desired outcomes.

Reflection

- How did it work?

- What will I do next time?

2.2 Defining a problem or opportunity statement

Why

Techniques like 'five whys' are valuable, but often different stakeholders will have subtly different perspectives over the problem we are trying to solve. Each of those perspectives may be valid, but it is important that there is a shared and agreed understanding of the problem we are trying to solve. If this does not happen, we may end up suggesting solutions that meet the needs of some stakeholders but fundamentally miss some core needs of another stakeholder group.

Knowledge briefing

> 'If I were given one hour to save the planet, I would spend 59 minutes defining the problem and one minute resolving it.'
>
> (Albert Einstein)

A problem statement is a concise yet precise paragraph or two which scopes out and articulates the problem. It is intended to create consensus, and validate that all relevant stakeholders agree that *this* is the particular problem or opportunity that we should be addressing. It should be as succinct as possible – a short and snappy problem statement will help ensure that it is easily read and digested. It does not need to cover every detail or nuance of the problem, however it *will* act as a useful guiding beacon for our further problem-solving activities.

Importantly, the problem statement should capture and articulate the known *root causes* of the problem and the *outcomes* that are desired.

Source: Michael D. Brown/Shutterstock

How

A suggested problem statement, as cited in *A Guide to the Business Analysis Body of Knowledge® (Guide®)*, v2, is listed below:

The problem of . . .	This section describes the nature of the problem. It will synthesise the information that has been obtained using 'five whys' and other techniques.
Affects . . .	Who does the problem primarily affect? Who are our important stakeholders?
The impact of which is . . .	What negative impact is the problem causing? How significant is that impact?
A successful solution would . . .	What outcomes would be achieved if we solved the problem?

Building on the example discussed in the previous section, a possible problem statement would be:

1. *The problem of* an increase in complaints due to an inability to process customer orders quickly enough during peak periods.

2. *Affects* our customers (who are disappointed), our warehouse staff (who cannot keep up with demand) and our call centre staff (who have to deal with unhappy customers).

3. *The impact of which is* cancelled orders, reputational damage and increased complaints – all of which lead to increased operational costs and a reduction in profits.

4. *A successful solution would* ensure that we can predict and manage demand, allowing us to dispatch orders in a timely fashion, leading to increased customer satisfaction, reduced operational costs and ultimately higher profits.

Combining these two techniques ('five whys' and the problem statement), we have moved beyond the temptation to jump towards a knee-jerk solution, and we have created a short, succinct statement that can guide further work. When creating problem statements of this type, it is normal to *iterate* – the first version almost certainly won't be correct. It can be useful to convene a workshop with the relevant stakeholders to finesse the wording and create a problem statement that everyone buys into. This can then become a useful guiding beacon for future work.

On some occasions, we'll be looking to address an *opportunity* rather than a problem. In these situations we can tweak the problem statement template to become an opportunity statement:

The opportunity of . . .	This section describes the nature of the opportunity, and why it should be pursued.
Would benefit . . .	Who would the opportunity primarily benefit? Who are the key stakeholders who would be positively impacted?
The impact of which is . . .	What positive impact would be created? How significant is that impact?
A successful solution would . . .	What outcomes would be achieved if the opportunity was leveraged?

Reflection

- How did it work?

- What will I do next time?

References

International Institute of Business Analysis (IIBA), 2009. *A Guide to the Business Analysis Body of Knowledge® (Guide®)*, v2. Toronto: IIBA.

2.3 Encourage divergent and convergent thinking

Why

As mentioned in the previous sections, often when examining a problem, our intuitive reaction is to pounce on a potential solution and then move towards implementing it. However, to ensure that the right outcomes are achieved, we have examined exploring the problem more holistically. It is useful to consider two different thinking styles that are relevant for problem solving.

Knowledge briefing

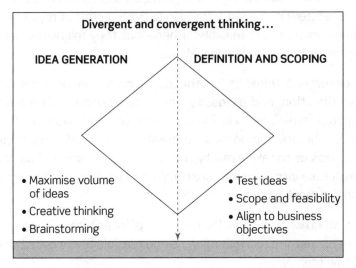

Divergent and convergent thinking...

IDEA GENERATION | DEFINITION AND SCOPING

- Maximise volume of ideas
- Creative thinking
- Brainstorming

- Test ideas
- Scope and feasibility
- Align to business objectives

Source: Adapted from Perspective, n.d. Creative Problem Solving – The Swiss Army Knife for BAs. London: presented at BA Conference Europe 2011

Divergent thinking encourages maximising the possible number of options or opportunities. For example, if you have ever held a brainstorm where you are generating ideas, you will have been thinking divergently. Crucially, when thinking divergently, it is beneficial to *turn off* (or at least turn down) our inner critic. When brainstorming, we might find that some of the ideas that are generated are outlandish and unlikely – yet at this point it is still useful to capture them. Even though they sound outlandish, we might later combine or adapt them in a way that makes them implementable – and had we let our inner critic self-censor them, we'd have lost out on this opportunity.

For example, if we were brainstorming how to solve traffic congestion in a city centre location, an idea such as 'build a second road network underground' might spring to mind. Clearly, this is an unlikely solution – but *seeing* this left-field idea might lead other people to contribute more feasible ideas. Perhaps the word 'underground' will resonate with somebody else, and an idea like 'incentivise use of existing underground trains/metros over road' might be captured. Another might focus on underground and 'flip' it to think about the *sky* – and perhaps contribute an idea such as 'move inter-city freight from road to light-aircraft'. It might be that these ideas aren't feasible either – but they might themselves spawn other, more feasible ideas.

Convergent thinking, on the other hand, encourages focus, prioritisation, and assessing the data at hand to find a single appropriate answer. Having generated tens or hundreds of ideas, it *is* ultimately important to create a short list. This thinking requires us to take a reality check and reign in some of our ideas. We'll take into account constraints and preferences to converge on the most likely possible solutions.

So, when we pare down the hundreds of ideas that were generated in a brainstorm to a manageable and feasible few, we are thinking convergently.

How

It can be useful to share the convergent/divergent thinking diagram with your stakeholders early on in the problem-solving process, and take the opportunity to explain the two different (but complementary) types of thinking. This allows us to clearly *signpost* the type of thinking that we're aiming for when working with stakeholders in meetings and workshops. This visual shorthand can ensure that everyone is on the same page.

Reflection

- How did it work?

- What will I do next time?

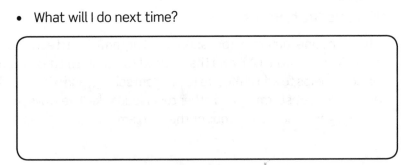

References

Perspectiv, n.d. *Creative Problem Solving – The Swiss Army Knife for BAs.* London: presented at BA Conference Europe 2011.

2.4 Get to the root of the problem

Why

As mentioned in Section 2.1, the 'five whys' technique helps us to achieve a rich understanding of the situation and will get us closer to the root of the problem. However, it is useful to use a variety of techniques to ensure that we gain a thorough understanding. This also provides us with the opportunity to validate our understanding of the problem with the relevant stakeholders.

A technique that can help is the fishbone diagram.

Source: Tuulijumala/Shutterstock

Knowledge briefing

The fishbone diagram (or Ishikawa diagram) is a technique conceived by Kaoru Ishikawa that is used to separate *cause* from *effect*. It helps to add structure to problem solving, and when used alongside brainstorming and other techniques like 'five whys', can help us get closer to the root of the problem.

How

A fishbone diagram is made up of a number of elements. The problem is placed on the right-hand side, and becomes the 'head' of the fish. This problem is then examined from a number of different angles, represented by the first set of 'bones' on the fish. In the example below, the following categories are used:

Category	Explanation	Example
Policies	Higher level organisational policies or decisions that affect or cause the problem	A recruitment freeze means that it isn't possible to replace key members of staff
Procedures	Processes and procedures that contribute to or cause the problem	Sales process is focussed on closing the sale, but does not always lead to accurate order detail being captured Before a response to a complaint can be issued, three reviews are required (leading to delays)
People	Issues related to people – including whether they have received the right level of training, whether there is sufficient resource and so forth	New staff have not been trained No staff appraisal process Lack of feedback provided to staff
Plant (Technology)	Plant and machinery – in a service environment or information-rich business, this is likely to relate to IT	IT system does not capture delivery date IT systems are not integrated, leading to manual re-keying (which is error prone)

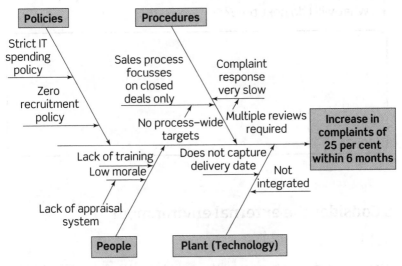

Source: Blackmetric Business Solutions

Brainstorms are held and other relevant investigation takes place to find likely causes. The relationships between each cause is shown, with multiple 'fishbones' pointing towards each other. Often primary, secondary and tertiary causes are shown. The fishbone diagram is most useful when we consider it to be an evolving document – one that we can add more information to as and when it becomes available.

As the fishbone diagram is created, we may find that some causes are more important or cause more impact than others. These are often the causes that warrant our immediate attention and investigation.

Reflection

- How did it work?

Think problem *before* solution

- What will I do next time?

> [blank box]

2.5 Consider the external environment

Why

Organisations don't exist within a bubble; they are affected by many significant factors which are outside of their direct control. As well as understanding the factors *within* your organisation that are contributing to the problem, it is worth considering the relevance of external factors too. For example, if sales revenues have dropped unexpectedly this may be due to a new competitor entering the market, or perhaps a competitor has started selling online and offering superior service. A useful technique to help us elicit and consider these external factors is STEEPLE.

Source: Marafona/Shutterstock

Knowledge briefing

STEEPLE is a technique that helps us examine the external environment. It helps us to uncover the social, technological, economic, environmental, political, legal and ethical factors that affect our industries. It is often used on a macro level as a strategic analysis technique, and can be used to find opportunities and threats in the business environment. However, it is also useful to consider these same environmental factors when problem solving. This may help us to identify *constraints* that we must adhere to (for example, a law or regulation that will affect how we solve the problem) as well as *opportunities* that can help us to solve the problem.

There are many variants of STEEPLE – you may also hear of PEST, STEP and PESTLE – these are all similar variants that achieve the same outcome. Other useful resources discussing complementary techniques can be found in the 'References and further reading' section.

How

When carrying out a STEEPLE analysis, an organisation's external environment is considered from the following perspectives:

Factor	Explanation
Social	Includes trends, fashions and social-cultural aspects of the business environments
Technological	Includes the availability of new and emerging technology
Economic	External economic factors such as a recession or an economic 'boom'
Environmental	Sustainability issues – for example, rising sea levels or hotter summers
Political	Any political factors from local, national or international government – may include trade sanctions, trading relationships and so on
Legal	Laws and regulations that must be complied with
Ethical	External considerations and pressures relating to ethical factors – for example, the increasing move away from 'sweat shop' environments

Often STEEPLE factors can be elicited by holding workshops, brainstorms as well as one-to-one conversations with relevant stakeholders. More formal research can also be useful, if there is time.

Building on our example of a mail-order retailer, some factors might include:

Factor	Examples
Social	• Increasing trend of customers moving away from cat-alogue-based shopping in favour of Internet-based shops presents a threat to the business • Increasing expectation of fast service has been created by new entrants to the industry: 28 days used to be the norm, now customers expect their deliveries the next day • Increasing awareness of consumer rights means that customers are more likely to return items • Increasing expectation of special offers/discounts, and the propensity for customers to use price compar-ison sites • Some customers are moving away from 'high-street' shopping, leading to an opportunity for catalogue retailers
Technological	• Availability of Internet and mobile app technology is a potential opportunity • New schedule and demand tracking systems are avail-able 'off the shelf' from software vendors • Analytic and tracking packages are available
Economic	• Recovery from a recession means increased disposable income • Competition in the mail-order retail market is cut-throat, with decreasing margins
Environmental	• Increasing focus on local shopping to avoid 'carbon footprint' of delivery • Increased focus on amount of packaging that is used in products and in particular parcels and deliveries
Political	• Increasing political pressure to resolve consumer complaints quickly • Increasing threat of 'heavy' regulation on distance selling
Legal	• Distance selling regulations constrain our sales process
Ethical	• Concern over minimum wage levels, with an increased focus on 'living wage'

A key factor to note with external analysis techniques like STEEPLE is that the organisation itself is unlikely to be able to directly *change* any of these factors. For example, our mail-order retailer can't change the distance selling regulations (although it might be able to influence them by working with other similar retailers and lobbying government). However, these factors both constrain how the organisation operates and also provide it with opportunities. It is crucial that these factors are kept in mind when later considering and evaluating potential solutions.

Reflection

- How did it work?

- What will I do next time?

2.6 Consider multiple perspectives on the problem

Why

As outlined in Section 2.1, there are likely to be a number of stakeholders who have an interest (or who are impacted by) the problem that we are examining. Different stakeholders are likely to have a slightly different perspective on the problem, and if the problem is complex, we might find that no single stakeholder understands the whole problem.

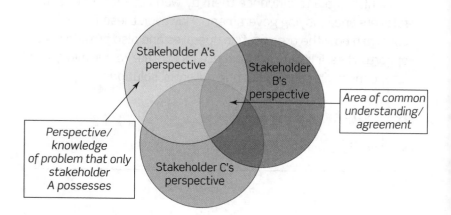

Knowledge briefing

There are a number of reasons why it is valuable to consider multiple perspectives on a problem:

- **Completeness:** Ensuring that the relevant stakeholders' views are represented will help ensure that we have as thorough an understanding of the problem as possible – and will ensure that we analyse and consider all the identifiable root causes. If we rely on just one perspective, we may miss significant and important details.

- **Coherence:** By involving stakeholders, we ensure that there is a coherent and agreed view of the problem we're trying to solve. We ensure that everyone is on the same page. We build out from the 'common view' in the centre of the previous diagram, and ensure views and expectations are aligned.

- **Commitment:** Consulting widely ensures that we have the opportunity to build rapport, understand people's views and (hopefully) gain commitment and buy-in to the problem-solving initiative.

How

The key is to actively build stakeholder identification and engagement into our problem-solving process. The stakeholder identification and categorisation technique referred to in Section 2.1 can help start this process, however throughout our problem-solving initiatives we should:

1. Ask 'Who else might be affected by this problem?' or 'Who might be interested in a solution to this problem?' Meet with them, hold workshops, ensure that they feel 'heard'.

2. Capture each stakeholder's view on what the problem *really* is.

3. Use techniques like 'five whys' to gain insight into the stakeholder's knowledge of the problem.

4. Where differences of opinion occur, bring the parties together to discuss them.

5. Use techniques like the fishbone diagram and the problem statement to facilitate group discussions over the scope and scale of the problem.

Reflection

- How did it work?

- What will I do next time?

2.7 Gain consensus and move forward

Why

Defining the problem is important, but it is crucial that we gain *consensus* over the scope, nature and root causes of the problem. This ensures that we have agreement on which root causes we'll address first, and which parts of the problem are in scope (and which might need to wait). Ensuring that there is early consensus will reduce the risk of conflict later – as we can be more confident that *everyone* has a common view on the problem we are trying to solve.

Knowledge briefing

Gaining consensus is as much art as science, but utilising the techniques already outlined in this chapter will help. In particular, building a fishbone diagram iteratively, after a number of conversations with the relevant stakeholders, can be useful. The diagram becomes a 'conversation starter' that can be used in a workshop to *validate* our understanding of the root causes. Often stakeholders will gain an appreciation of other perspectives, and this can help avoid conflict later. It is even possible to highlight the fishbone diagram to show elements of the problem that are/aren't in the immediate scope of our problem-solving initiative.

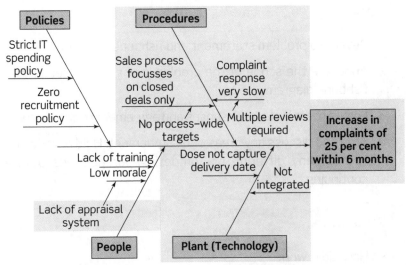

Shaded areas are in the scope of our problem-solving initiative

The problem statement is also a useful tool for gaining consensus. This concise yet precise artefact can often lead to much wrangling over precise wording. Although this can feel inconvenient, it is often very useful in the long run. We may find, for example, that a particular stakeholder objects to the use of the word 'customer' in the problem statement, preferring instead 'retail customer'. This might seem like a pedantic change, but it may actually be quite significant. It may highlight that there are different *types* of customer, and this will alert us to the need to investigate further.

A well-written problem statement will be extremely useful throughout the problem-solving initiative. It is useful to keep a printed copy handy in meetings, and put it in the centre of the table. As we start to discuss more detailed requirements and potential solutions with our stakeholders, we can ensure that each requirement raised *contributes* towards solving the problem. If it doesn't, then maybe it isn't a requirement that we need to consider. Or, if it is a genuine requirement, perhaps the problem has expanded (and we need to revisit the problem statement)! This will help us keep on track and on scope, and will help avoid scope-creep.

How

1. Develop a problem statement and fishbone diagram.

2. Annotate the scope of the problem being addressed on the fishbone diagram.

3. Ensure there is clear consensus and agreement over the scope.

4. Stop and discuss any areas of disagreement. Hold a workshop to hear any differing or competing perspectives before continuing.

Reflection

- How did it work?

- What will I do next time?

Chapter 3

Defining the outcomes: what does success look like?

3.1 Encourage outcome-based thinking

It is very easy for us and our stakeholders to inadvertently fall back into solution-oriented thinking *before* we have fully defined the problem. This may lead to us arbitrarily selecting a solution, and may have the unfortunate effect of closing down further discussion about other potentially better or more suitable solutions.

Shifting from solution to outcome-based thinking can be helpful. In Chapter 2 we discussed understanding and analysing the current state – this is only part of the picture. It is also crucial that we define the destination or 'future state' that we want to achieve. It is important that we define what success looks like, and this chapter examines this idea in more detail.

A useful first step towards outcome-based thinking is to highlight, and re-frame, any solution-biased statements that we hear. For example:

Solution-biased statement	Re-framed response
We need a new computer system so that we can respond to customers more quickly	If I understand you correctly, the core aim here is to respond to customers more quickly, and you've mentioned that a new computer system is one way of achieving this. What else about a potential solution is important to you? Are there any other goals or outcomes that you are aiming to achieve? Outcome: Respond to customers more quickly

Defining the outcomes: what does success look like?

Source: Scrugglegreen/Shutterstock

Do this

Spot solution-biased statements. Re-frame these statements, focussing on the outcome rather than the solution. This is a useful way for us to gain an initial understanding of the desired business outcome – this understanding can be refined as the problem-solving initiative continues.

3.2 Start with the end in mind: define critical success factors

Critical success factors (CSFs) can be defined as:

> *'The areas in which an organisation must succeed in order to achieve positive organisational performance.'*
>
> (Paul, Cadle and Yeates, 2014)

CSFs are often defined at a macro (organisational) level, but are equally relevant at project or problem-solving initiative level. They help us to define the goals of the initiative, and help us clarify why it is worth solving the problem at all.

CSFs are generally qualitative, and initially we don't need to define how they will be measured. Example CSFs might include:

- A world-class reputation for flawless service
- Accurate dispatch and logistics

The CSFs show the broad aims of the project, and it is important they are aligned with any overarching organisational CSFs and the company's strategy.

Making them measurable is important, and this is discussed in the next section.

Source: Olivier Le Moal/Shutterstock

Do this

Elicit critical success factors (CSFs) through workshops, brainstorming and one-to-one conversations. Ask questions like:

'How will we know when the problem is solved?'

'What specific outcomes are important for you?'

'What will the organisation look and feel like once we've achieved our outcomes?'

'Is there anything else we need to achieve?'

'What do we need to avoid?'

'What does success look, sound and feel like?'

3.3 Make it measurable with key performance indicators

It is important that any critical success factors (CSFs) are made measurable. This can be achieved by defining relevant and measurable key performance indicators.

Defining the outcomes: what does success look like?

Key performance indicators (KPIs) can be defined as:

> '[The] specific areas of performance that are monitored in order to assess the performance of an organisation. Key performance indicators are often identified in order to monitor progress of the critical success factors.'
>
> (Paul, Cadle and Yeates, 2014)

As implied by the definition, KPIs are often applied at an organisational level – but it can be equally useful to define them for a project, problem or problem-solving initiative. The relationship between KPIs and CSFs is illustrated in the diagram below:

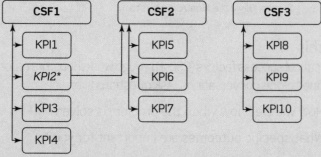

In this example KPI2 helps measure the progress of both CSF1 and CSF2

Every CSF should have at least one KPI – and one KPI may relate to one or more CSFs. Each KPI should be unambiguous, so that it is extremely clear how measurement can be made.

Do this
Work with stakeholders to define what they would measure to determine whether a successful outcome has been achieved. For each CSF define at least one (but normally more than one) KPI.

3.4 Attain balance with the balanced business scorecard

In the previous sections we have discussed defining the required outcomes using critical success factors (CSFs) and key performance indicators (KPIs). There is an inherent danger, as soon as we start discussing measurement, that we might inadvertently encourage unexpected outcomes. As the old expression goes: 'You get what you *inspect* not what you *expect*'.

If we focus our measures on one specific area of performance we might inadvertently affect others. For example, if a call centre manager is instructed to reward their staff for achieving an average call length of three minutes (and lambasts those that do not achieve this) they may find that they get *lots* of sub three-minute calls, but lots of very unhappy customers (as the call centre staff, quite understandably, are focussing on doing the *quickest* thing rather than the *best* thing for the customer).

It is therefore important that we achieve *balance.* In the call centre example above, it may be useful to have other measures – perhaps focussing on customer satisfaction – as well as call length.

A useful way to achieve this balance is the balanced business scorecard. Ensuring that we consider each angle of the balanced business scorecard will ensure that we help achieve equilibrium.

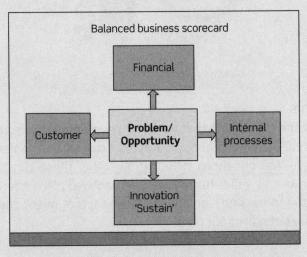

Do this

When defining CSFs or KPIs, or shortly after, use the balanced business scorecard to ensure there is relevant balance and coverage of each angle. You may want to adjust the scorecard adding additional factors that are relevant for your industry or domain.

3.5 Revisit and consider constraints

Whatever the organisation and problem we are examining, there are likely to be a range of constraints that narrow down the potential solutions that can be considered. Budget is likely to be limited, and this may mean that we are searching for a 'silver' or 'bronze' rather than 'solid gold' solution.

We discussed identifying constraints in Section 1.6 – as the problem-solving initiative continues it is important that we *revisit* constraints, ensure they are still valid, and ensure that any solution will fit within them.

Source: Sashkin/Shutterstock

Do this

Revisit the constraints that have been uncovered to ensure they are all still valid and that nothing in the external environment has changed. Ask questions including: 'Are all of these constraints still true and valid, from your perspective?', 'Are there any constraints missing?' and 'What other factors might there be that are outside of our control?'

3.6 Ensuring organisational alignment

It is important that we don't carry out our problem-solving activities in a bubble. Organisations normally have a stated vision/mission, a set of objectives and strategies. It is important that we align our problem-solving activities with the overall organisational objectives/strategies. This may shape the solutions that we choose – after all, we wouldn't want our initiative to pull in a direction that opposes the overall organisational strategy!

A useful way of encouraging thinking about strategic alignment can be to add a strategic alignment statement to our previously defined problem statement. This involves adding two lines:

This aligns with our stated strategy by . . .
And would help us meet our objectives of . . .

Adding these two lines helps us illustrate and maintain alignment to the organisational level objectives and strategy.

Source: A1Stock/Shutterstock

Do this
Be aware of your organisation's vision, mission strategy and objectives. Add a strategic alignment statement to each problem statement that is defined.

3.7 Assess different perspectives on outcomes

Different people in our organisation may have different views on the outcomes being pursued in a particular problem-solving initiative. If these differences are not addressed, there is a real danger that we'll end up disappointing one or more stakeholder groups.

The techniques discussed in the previous sections in this chapter will help to create a useful conversation around outcomes – they may highlight any tacit disagreement that exists. In some cases stakeholders may have varying, but complementary views, on what is trying to be achieved. It can be useful to map the desired outcomes/benefits, to ensure that they fit together. An example diagram showing dependencies is shown below.

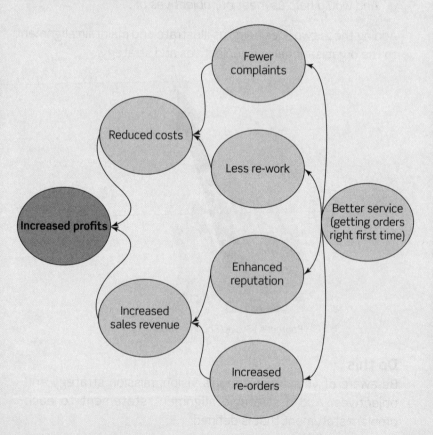

Do this

Ensure that you fully understand what each key stakeholder group is trying to achieve out of the problem-solving initiatives. Highlight any conflicts and work with the team to reconcile or resolve them. Ensure that the dependencies between outcomes/benefits are understood.

BIG PICTURE

3. Defining the outcomes: what does success look like?

3.1 Encourage outcome-based thinking

Why

In Chapter 2, we discussed the importance of focussing on the problem before considering or selecting a solution. A rich understanding of the problem helps guide us towards the most appropriate solution. However, understanding the problem in isolation is rarely enough. As well as understanding what we're trying to *get away from* (the problem) we also need to understand the *destination we're wanting to arrive at* (the outcome).

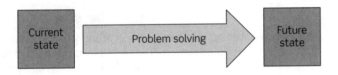

Outcome-based thinking encourages us to forget about what the solution looks like (for now), but focus on what the solution will deliver. It helps us answer the question 'How will things be different after this problem is solved?'

Knowledge briefing

Clearly defined outcomes help us to understand and articulate what our stakeholders want to achieve by implementing a solution and solving a problem. It helps us move away from the natural tendency to think in solutions.

The 'five whys' technique that was mentioned earlier can be useful for eliciting outcomes, as well as root causes. In fact, when using 'five whys' to determine root causes, it is likely that our stakeholders will mention desired *outcomes* too – and it is useful to capture these.

Even when people are clear about the outcomes that they are aiming for, they will often (unconsciously) tie the outcome to a pre-conceived solution. It can be useful to *re-frame* existing statements, and play them back to our stakeholders to make sure we understand correctly.

Some examples are shown below:

Solution-biased statement	Re-framed response
I need a car so that I can get to work on time	So, assuming I have understood correctly, your ultimate aim is to get to work on time, and you've noted that a car is one way of achieving this. Are there any other outcomes or constraints we need to know about? Outcome: Get to work on time
We need a new computer system so that we can respond to customers more quickly	If I understand you correctly, the core aim here is to respond to customers more quickly, and you've mentioned that a new computer system is one way of achieving this. What else about a potential solution is important to you? Are there any other goals or outcomes that you are aiming to achieve? Outcome: Respond to customers more quickly
We need ten new members of staff so that we can scale up to meet an upcoming peak	The main outcome, if I understand correctly, is to ensure we can meet an anticipated upcoming peak in demand – or presumably it would be even better if we could manage and level that demand, if possible, is that correct? Outcome: Scale up to meet an upcoming peak OR manage and level demand

How

1. Use a problem statement (see Section 2.2) (particularly the final line 'A successful solution would . . . ') to create a conversation about outcomes.

2. Throughout the problem-solving process, encourage people to think about *problems* and *outcomes* before *solutions.*

3. Re-frame solution-biased statements and check for a common understanding on the desired outcomes.

4. Define critical success factors and key performance indicators, as discussed later in this chapter.

5. Use the balanced business score card to ensure the required outcomes are balanced.

Reflection

- How did it work?

- What will I do next time?

3.2 Start with the end in mind: define critical success factors

Why

A useful way to encourage, enhance and clarify our outcome-based thinking is to assess what aspects are *critical* for the success of the problem-solving initiative. This involves assessing the outcomes that *must* be achieved in order that the problem is considered solved.

It can be very useful to articulate these high-priority outcomes as *critical success factors (CSFs)*.

Source: Olivier Le Moal/Shutterstock

Knowledge briefing

Critical success factors (CSFs) can be defined as:

> *'The areas in which an organisation must succeed in order to achieve positive organisational performance.'*
>
> (Paul, Cadle and Yeates, 2014)

As implied by the definition, CSFs are often defined at an organisational level, and often form an important gauge of whether the organisation's strategy is working effectively. As well as utilising CSFs at a macro level, across an entire organisation, it is also possible to utilise them at a more detailed level for a particular problem, project or problem-solving initiative.

CSFs are generally *qualitative.* That is, they don't have to be directly measurable or immediately quantifiable. CSFs might include:

- Excellent customer service
- Sufficient revenue and profits (without yet specifying the amounts of revenue and profit)
- World-class reputation for flawless service
- Best-in class logistics
- Accurate dispatch

Defining CSFs helps set direction and highlights the critical business outcomes that we are looking to achieve without getting caught up into the detail of how they will be measured. Of course, we do ultimately need to make CSFs measurable – this is achieved by assigning key performance indicators (KPIs), which is discussed in the next section.

How

Critical success factors can be elicited by liaising with our stakeholders, through workshops, brainstorming and one-to-one conversations. Useful questions to ask include:

'How will we know when the problem is solved?'

'What specific outcomes are important for you?'

'What will the organisation look and feel like once we've achieved our outcomes?'

'Is there anything else we need to achieve?'

'What do we need to avoid?'

'What does success look, sound and feel like?'

Capture the responses as concise bullet-pointed statements. It can be useful to use the balanced business scorecard, which is discussed later in this section, when considering CSFs as this provides useful categories to frame our discussions. It is also important that we ensure the CSFs (and any accompanying KPIs) for the problem-solving initiative are suitably aligned to the overarching organisational CSFs and objectives – i.e. it is important that our problem-solving initiative is aligned with the wider organisational strategy.

Reflection

- How did it work?

- What will I do next time?

References

Paul, D., Cadle, J. and Yeates, D. (eds), 2014. *Business Analysis.* Third Edition. Swindon: BCS.

3.3 Make it measurable with key performance indicators

Why

Critical success factors help us define the broad and important outcomes that we are aiming to achieve with our problem-solving initiative. Perhaps we are aiming to improve the experience for our customers, or reduce costs. These factors will act as guiding beacons throughout our entire problem-solving initiative, helping us to ensure that we select and implement the right solution.

However, as mentioned in the previous section, CSFs are not directly measurable. It is therefore useful to define and pin key performance indicators (KPIs) and targets to our CSFs.

Knowledge briefing

Key performance indicators (KPIs) can be defined as:

> '[The] specific areas of performance that are monitored in order to assess the performance of an organisation. Key performance indicators are often identified in order to monitor progress of the critical success factors.'

> (Paul, Cadle and Yeates, 2014)

Every CSF should have at least one KPI – and it is usual for CSFs to have *many* KPIs. Additionally, in some circumstances, one KPI may relate to more than one CSF.

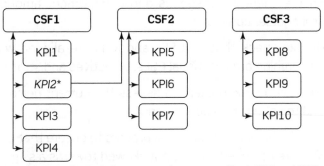

* In this example KPI2 helps measure the progress of both CSF1 and CSF2

If our CSF was world-class reputation for flawless service, we may consider KPIs including:

- Survey results amongst customers (80 per cent agreeing that our organisation has an excellent or world class reputation for service).
- Survey results amongst random members of the public (who may or may not be customers) with 70 per cent agreeing that our organisation has an excellent or world class reputation for service.
- Complaint rates should be lower than 1 in 1000 transactions (note, this is a 'proxy measure' as it does not directly relate to *reputation,* but is based on the assumption that if complaints are low, reputation will be good).

The KPIs that are chosen will help refine the CSF and make it extremely clear the specific progress that is being pursued with the problem-solving initiative.

How

1. Take each CSF and ask 'How could we measure this?'
2. Look for multiple, complementary measures.
3. Ensure that each KPI is actually measurable. Is the data available? Can it be measured reliably? If not, perhaps it should be refined.
4. Ensure each KPI is unambiguous and clearly understood.
5. Ensure there is consensus and commitment amongst the stakeholder community.
6. Double-check that all CSFs and KPIs are aligned with any overarching organisational CSFs, objectives and strategy.
7. Work with stakeholders to assess the current performance, and to set a future benchmark.
8. Use the balanced business scorecard to ensure that CSFs and KPIs are balanced and are not skewed towards a single area – this is discussed in the next section.

Reflection

- How did it work?

[ ]

- What will I do next time?

[ ]

References

Paul, D., Cadle, J. and Yeates, D. (eds), 2014. *Business Analysis.* Third Edition. Swindon: BCS.

3.4 Attain balance with the balanced business scorecard

Why

It is crucial that sufficient thought is put into CSFs and KPIs – else we might end up inadvertently incentivising and attaining the wrong types of outcome. We might get exactly what we've *asked* for, even though (in retrospect) this isn't what we *wanted and needed*. Building upon our mail-order retail company example: We might want to ensure that 99 per cent of parcels are dispatched within

24 hours – however achieving this would be of little use if 20 per cent of those parcels were incorrectly packed (leading to the items being damaged in transit!). There have been high-profile headlines in recent years indicating that targets and league tables can have unintended consequences and outcomes if we are not careful.

To avoid these types of dilemma, it is important to *balance* our CSFs and KPIs. A useful tool to help us achieve this is the balanced business scorecard.

Knowledge briefing

The balanced scorecard was originally created by Kaplan and Norton, and is further described in the book *The Balanced Scorecard: Translating Strategy Into Action* (Kaplan and Norton, 1996). A balanced business scorecard is often used to balance the CSFs and KPIs of an entire organisation. However, we can equally use this to balance the CSFs or KPIs of a particular problem-solving initiative:

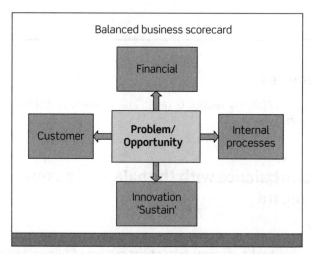

Source: Adapted from Kaplan, R.S. and Norton, D.P., 1996. *The Balanced Scorecard: Translating Strategy Into Action.* Boston, MA: Harvard Business School Press

The balanced business scorecard encourages us to consider four aspects: financial, customer, internal processes, and learning and growth/innovation (which we will call 'sustain'). It is important to consider all of these areas to achieve balance – if we focus purely on one area, we may cause inadvertent negative impacts (e.g. focussing purely on finance might lead to negative impacts on customer service and innovation through overly tough cost-saving exercises). When defining CSFs and KPIs, we may find that out stakeholders initially focus in just one or two of these areas – by consciously considering the scorecards, we can ensure that we achieve 'balance'.

Each section of the scorecard is explained below, with example CSFs and KPIs provided.

Aspect	Relevance for problem solving	Example CSFs	Example KPIs
Finance	This aspect relates to the financial performance of the organisation. What will be different financially when the problem is solved?	Increased sales revenue Increased profit Avoid costs	• Increase in sales revenue of x per cent by the end of next year in product line y • Profit margin of x per cent • Net profit of £x • Cost of sales reduces to x per cent
Customer	What will solving the problem mean for the customer?	Excellent customer service	• 95 per cent of our customers indicate they'd recommend us to a friend (measured by annual survey) • 1 in 10 customers take up our 'refer a friend' initiative • Complaints less than 1 in 1000 transactions
Internal processes	What internal processes do we need to consider or measure? This can include manual processes, IT, staff related aspects and so on	Best-in class Warehouse and dispatch capability	• 99.9 per cent accuracy in picking and packing • 99 per cent of packages dispatched within 24 hours of order

Defining the outcomes: what does success look like?

Aspect	Relevance for problem solving	Example CSFs	Example KPIs
Innovation 'sustain'	Traditionally, this section of the balanced business scorecard focusses on innovation or learning and growth. In the context of a problem it is worth thinking about sustainability – or, more specifically, how do we ensure that the problem stays solved. What measures might indicate that the problem has recurred?	Protect and retain our position in the market	• Market share of x per cent is retained • Complaint rate of less than 1 in 1000 transactions

How

It can be useful to start by eliciting CSFs/KPIs from stakeholders via an open brainstorm – ask questions like: 'How do we know we've been successful?' and 'How can we measure that success?' Next, categorise these factors onto the balanced business scorecard. Next, it is useful to look for gaps and use the scorecard to prompt further CSFs and KPIs. This is often an iterative process, and it may take several rounds of discussion to refine and finalise.

Once the balanced scorecard looks complete, it is worth validating by asking questions such as 'What is missing?' and 'Is there anything here that could be misinterpreted or misunderstood?' It is additionally worth ensuring all key stakeholders are committed and bought-into the metrics that the scorecard defines. Finally, it is worth noting that the categories on the balanced scorecard, whilst very useful, can be *flexed* and added to. They are useful suggestions, but it can be useful to increment and add to these to make the scorecard as 'real' for our organisation as possible.

Reflection

- How did it work?

```
┌──────────────────────────────────────────────┐
│                                                │
│                                                │
│                                                │
│                                                │
│                                                │
│                                                │
└──────────────────────────────────────────────┘
```

- What will I do next time?

```
┌──────────────────────────────────────────────┐
│                                                │
│                                                │
│                                                │
│                                                │
│                                                │
│                                                │
└──────────────────────────────────────────────┘
```

References

Kaplan, R.S. and Norton, D.P., 1996. *The Balanced Scorecard: Translating Strategy Into Action.* Boston, MA: Harvard Business School Press.

3.5 Revisit and consider constraints

Why

Having defined the problem and defined the *outcomes* that we are aiming to achieve, we will soon be able to start assessing potential solutions. However, in every situation there will be constraints that affect the solutions to the problem that are feasible or appropriate. It may be that only a certain amount of budget is available, or that a solution must be implemented within a certain timeframe. There may even be technical constraints that prevent us from changing certain IT systems (or make it much less attractive to do so).

We discussed the identification of constraints in Section 1.6. However, it is important that we revisit these constraints to ensure that they are still valid, and so that we can ensure that any solution that we recommend will fit within them.

Knowledge briefing

As outlined in Section 1.6, the types of constraint that we may encounter are varied and can include the following:

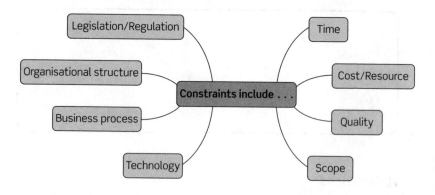

How

In Section 1.6, we discussed a constraints log, with the following suggested information being the minimum to collect and capture about each constraint.

ID	Constraint	Rationale	Owner	Last updated	Due for review
C01	The solution must be delivered within a budget of £10,000	A fixed budget has been agreed; there will be insufficient financial benefits to warrant exceeding this budget	Steven D	6th Dec	6th Mar

ID	Constraint	Rationale	Owner	Last updated	Due for review
C02	Any technological element must interface with an IAL SD/500 Series server	Our core customer database is stored on a HAL SD/500 Series, and a strategic architectural decision has been made to ensure all components interface or are compatible with this	Jayne B	2nd Nov	2nd Feb

As the problem-solving initiative continues, it is important to revisit these constraints. Ask whether they are still valid – sometimes an internal or external change may have rendered one or more of our constraints obsolete. Perhaps a major upgrade project has been commissioned, which changes our technical constraints (or imposes new ones). Perhaps a law has changed, meaning additional regulatory constraints need to come into our focus.

It is worth discussing these points openly with stakeholders. A good time to revisit these factors is when defining CSFs and KPIs (as discussed in earlier sections), or shortly after defining them. Having started to define the required outcomes, it is valuable to ask 'What is fixed and *can't* change?' Using the constraints log as a conversation starter, it is also illuminating to ask questions like:

'Has anything changed in our business environment since we last discussed constraints?'

'Are all of these constraints still true and valid, from your perspective?'

'Are there any constraints missing?'

'What *can't* we change?'

'What is beyond the pale?'

'What must stay the same?'

'What is limited?'

And:

'What other factors might there be that are outside of our control?'

It can also be valuable to look back at the STEEPLE factors discussed in Section 2.5.

Reflection

- How did it work?

```
┌─────────────────────────────────────────────────────┐
│                                                     │
│                                                     │
│                                                     │
│                                                     │
│                                                     │
└─────────────────────────────────────────────────────┘
```

- What will I do next time?

```
┌─────────────────────────────────────────────────────┐
│                                                     │
│                                                     │
│                                                     │
│                                                     │
│                                                     │
└─────────────────────────────────────────────────────┘
```

3.6 Ensuring organisational alignment

Why

As well as focussing on solving the problem, it is also useful to ensure that the problem-solving activity aligns with the organisation's vision/ mission, objective and strategies. It would be *very* unfortunate to solve the problem in a way that is out of kilter with the direction that the organisation is taking! Focussing on this alignment will ensure that we are solving the *right* problem in the *right* way.

Let's take a hypothetical example and imagine we are working in a hotel, and there is a problem as room keys continually go missing (as guests forget to return them). One solution might be to insist that guests hand their key in at reception each time they leave the hotel – even during their stay. However, this would be very inconvenient, and if the hotel was pursuing a strategy of differentiation (through provision of customer service) then it would likely cause problems. Customers would be expecting exceptional service, and would see the request to hand in their key in as unusual and unwieldy. This could lead to unhappy customers and a rise in complaints, and is out of kilter with the organisation's strategic positioning. Of course, in a budget hotel, which competes purely on price (rather than service) this might be a more palatable solution.

Source: Jojje/Shutterstock

Knowledge briefing

In the 2011 book *Good Strategy/Bad Strategy*, Rumelt describes strategy as:

'A cohesive response to an important challenge.'

(Rumelt, 2011)

He goes on to differentiate strategy from stand-alone activities:

'Unlike a stand-alone decision or a goal, a strategy is a coherent set of analyses, concepts, policies, arguments, and actions that respond to a high-stakes challenge.'

(Rumelt, 2011)

A significant part of this definition is its mention of coherence and cohesiveness. The projects, tasks and processes undertaken by an organisation should all be aligned with its strategies, and should help it strive towards its vision.

How

In order to ensure our problem-solving activities are aligned, it is important to ensure that we *know* what our organisation's stated vision, mission, objectives and strategies are. If these are not clear, then it is well worth spending time seeking further clarification. Those who set strategy are often very happy to spend time explaining it, and usually welcome curiosity. They will normally be extremely happy to answer questions and provide clarity.

If there *isn't* a clear strategy – or if the organisation has never consciously articulated strategy – then our time may be better spent helping to crystallise and document this first. This is a significant and effortful task, and the activities involved are beyond the scope of this book – however some helpful resources are found in the 'References and further reading' section.

Once we have established a clear view of the organisation's strategies, we should keep these firmly in our minds – and encourage our stakeholders to do the same too. They act as an organisational compass, and we should be able to identify a clear line-of-sight between our activities and the organisation's stated strategies. If we are unable to relate our activities to one or more of the organisation's strategies then it is a red flag, and there is a real possibility we have gone off on the wrong track. (Or, alternatively, if our activities really *are* necessary then perhaps the organisational strategy needs revisiting – which can be a much bigger endeavour.)

It can be useful to add a strategic alignment statement to our problem statement. This is achieved by adding two additional sentences:

This aligns with our stated strategy by . . .
And would help us meet our objectives of . . .

These two lines help connect our problem statement to strategy, and act as a useful prompt. Ultimately, the key is to keep coherence, and keep traceability between our activities and the organisation's aims, goals and strategy.

Reflection

- How did it work?

[ ]

- What will I do next time?

[ ]

References

Rumelt, R., 2011. *Good Strategy/Bad Strategy: The Difference and Why it Matters*. London: Profile Books.

3.7 Assess different perspectives on outcomes

Why

It is possible that different people within our organisations will have subtly different (and sometimes *significantly different*) perspectives on outcomes that are being pursued and the benefits they are trying to realise. Left unchecked, we could end up in a situation where we solve a problem for *some* stakeholders, but other stakeholders don't attain the outcomes they are looking for. This would lead to disappointment, and a feeling (for some) that the problem hadn't really been solved at all.

Knowledge briefing

Throughout this chapter, we have discussed defining *outcomes* that need to be achieved. As we work with different stakeholders, it is likely that different opinions over these outcomes will begin to surface. Defining outcomes helps us to highlight any differences in expectations, and also to understand whether different stakeholders are pursuing subtly different motives and objectives.

Drawing on the mail-order catalogue business we have discussed in previous chapters, we may find that the following stakeholders are pursing the following outcomes:

- Sales Director: 'I want us to be able to *provide better service,* so we *enhance our reputation* and *increase sales revenue.'*
- Head of Customer Operations: 'I want us to be able to *provide better service, first time every time* so that we have *fewer complaints* and *less re-work.'*
- Managing Director: 'I want us to *provide better service* which should lead to an *increased repeat order rate.* My ultimate goal is to *increase our profit* whilst delighting our customers.'

The different stakeholders have subtly different, but in this case compatible, views on the outcome being achieved. It is important to capture and reconcile these, and capture any dependencies between them. This is illustrated in the example below.

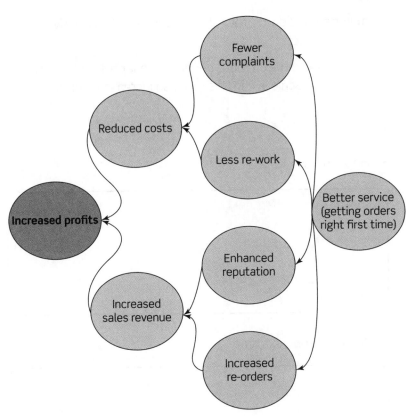

How

We can compare perspectives whilst following the other steps outlined in this book.

1. Elicit outcomes, CSFs and KPIs.

2. Use the balanced scorecard to prompt further discussion.

3. Use 'benefits map' style diagram (similar to the one shown above) to show the dependencies between desired outcomes.

4. Highlight any outcomes that cannot be met (perhaps as they fall outside of the agreed scope of the problem-solving initiative) and clearly manage expectations. These 'outliers'

may be candidates for future problem-solving activity, or a future project.

5. Trace back to the ultimate *benefit* or *benefits* that the initiative is trying to achieve – in this case, an increase in profits.

Reflection

*   How did it work?

*   What will I do next time?

Chapter 4

Assessing scope and impact

4.1 The danger of 'scope creep'

As problem-solving projects or initiatives progress, there is a tendency for their scope to inadvertently increase. Stakeholders mention other related (but different) problems, and there is a desire to fix those too. Care must be taken not to try to 'boil the ocean' – if the scope of our project or initiative is not controlled, we may end up taking on more work than we have the resources to handle. This may lead to a situation where we can't solve the *original* problem we were looking at – or even worse we may run out of time or budget leaving only half a job done.

It is crucial not only to ensure that there is early agreement on scope, but also to ensure that it is carefully controlled and managed throughout. Of course, our boundaries of scope *may* need to change sometimes – we may discover a new relevant situation, system or process – but this should always be assessed and the decision to include it (or not) should be a conscious one.

Source: Tan Kian Khoon/Shutterstock

Do this

Use the problem statement, CSFs and KPIs throughout the problem-solving initiative to keep a laser-like focus on scope. Ensure that any proposed deviations are consciously discussed, assessed, with a decision made over whether or not to pursue them.

4.2 Know the difference: impacted, interested and involved

As we assess and control the scope of a problem (and later a solution), it is important that we continually assess our stakeholder landscape. It is often the stakeholders who are most *interested* in a problem (or its potential solution) who are most visible – however there may be others who need careful consideration. Some stakeholders may be *impacted* by a potential solution – perhaps there will be a new process or system that they need to adopt. Others may need to be *involved* with the detailed problem analysis or solution deployment – although they might not know it yet!

Spreading our stakeholder analysis net wide, and revisiting our analysis regularly, will ensure that we do not inadvertently miss an important piece of the puzzle. It will also enable us to engage the right people at the right time, and enable us to build rapport with those that will ultimately make the solution work.

Source: Lord and Leverett/Pearson Education Ltd

Do this

Regularly revisit your stakeholder analysis and management plan. Consider the problem from multiple perspectives and through various lenses. Ask questions like:

Who has an interest in solving this problem?

What other processes, systems and people might be impacted?

Who or what sits just outside the boundaries of our problem scope? Might we inadvertently impact them?

4.3 Understand the problem situation

In a previous section we have discussed working with our colleagues and stakeholders to create a fishbone diagram (see Section 2.4). This is rarely a 'one and done' activity.

The first iteration of the fishbone diagram often usefully signposts areas that warrant further investigation. In order to uncover further detail, it is necessary to carry out further investigation.

There are a number of investigative techniques that we could use to probe further into the problem situation. These techniques include meeting/interviewing relevant and knowledgeable stakeholders, holding workshops and brainstorming sessions and observing processes happening so that we can see the problem situation with our own eyes. Each of these techniques helps bring us closer to the detail, and enriches our understanding of the situation.

As we uncover this richer level of detail, the fishbone diagram we created earlier can be added to incrementally, capturing more detailed root causes and supporting information.

Source: dadabosh/Shutterstock

Do this
Use investigative techniques such as meetings/interviews, workshops, brainstorming and observation to understand the detailed problem situation. Incrementally add to the fishbone diagram created earlier.

4.4 Find the roles and goals

As discussed previously, it is important to identify stakeholders who are impacted by the problem, as well as stakeholders who would benefit from (or be impacted by) any solution. Building on this idea further, and zooming in to focus on a specific subset of people, it is useful to understand those stakeholders who are wanting to achieve something with the solution that we implement – those who will use it or be involved in some way. These stakeholders will have a 'role' in the ongoing operation of the solution.

Having established the 'role' we can then go on to consider their 'goals' – what is it that they want to achieve (or how will they be involved) with the solution once it is rolled out? An example might be a *customer* that has a goal of *place order*. Perhaps a

Marketing Manager has a goal to *schedule marketing campaign.* Identifying the roles and goals involved or impacted helps us refine and validate scope, and also helps us to understand areas which might need to change or adapt in order to solve the problem.

Source: Mack2happy/Shutterstock

Do this

Identify the roles and goals and create a list to guide future analysis of the problem.

4.5 Make it visual with a business use case model

A business use case model is a way of visually depicting the roles and goals we captured earlier. A business use case model has four main symbols, as illustrated in the figure below.

The business use case model helps communicate the processes/ services that are involved in the problem, and helps visually communicate scope. It can later be built upon or annotated to show the areas that are being changed or impacted.

Symbol	Description	Role/Goal
	Business (external) actor: An entity *outside* of the business or organisation being analysed or discussed. This can include a person/team (role) or even an external IT system. Examples might include: customer, partner, vendor/supplier etc.	Role
	Worker (internal) actor: A role *within* the business or organisation being analysed or discussed. Examples might include: customer services, sales, manufacturing etc.	Role
	Business use case: An interaction between an actor and the business or organisation being analysed and discussed. This should be described as a short 'verb noun' phrase, describing a goal that the actor is trying to attain. Examples might include: place order, return item, query bill etc.	Goal
→	**Communication (association):** Shows which actors interact with which business use cases.	Links roles to goals

Source: These symbols are an extension to the Unified Modelling Language and are adapted from Podeswa, H., 2009. *The Business Analyst's Handbook*. Boston: Course Technology PTR, a part of Cengage Learning

Do this

Refine the roles and goals that you captured earlier into a business use case model. Validate this with your stakeholders to ensure that it is complete, and use it to create conversations over other potential contributing factors to the problem or potential solutions.

4.6 Set the priorities

Our problem-solving initiative is likely to be constrained by factors including budget and time. We'll have a limited amount of money or resources, and a limited timeframe in which to get our solution implemented. In some cases we might find that we don't have sufficient resource to solve *every* facet of the problem, but we do have sufficient resources to solve *part* of the problem. In situations like this it is important to consider which parts of the solution have the potential to deliver most value – or, to put this differently, which are the highest priority.

Prioritisation can take many forms, but it can be useful to consider the *goals* that we uncovered earlier – particularly if we elaborated these into a business use case diagram. Each business use case can be considered in turn to decide which warrant inclusion in the problem-solving initiative, and which can wait. Some may be consciously excluded from scope altogether to save time and money.

Source: Worker/Shutterstock

Do this

Consider the goals that are defined earlier (or business use cases that appear on the diagram) and assess which are central to the problem-solving initiative. Use a prioritisation scale – perhaps high/medium/low, or a more formal scale, to compare the relative importance. Focus on the potential value that would be delivered by a solution in each area.

4.7 Set the boundaries of scope

Once the prioritisation exercise discussed in the previous section has taken place, a more granular view on the solution scope will have been defined. This can be described visually by physically drawing a boundary of scope around the business use case diagram – showing those business use cases that are in or out of scope. An example is shown below, with the shaded areas being in scope – and those not shaded being *out* of scope of investigation.

111

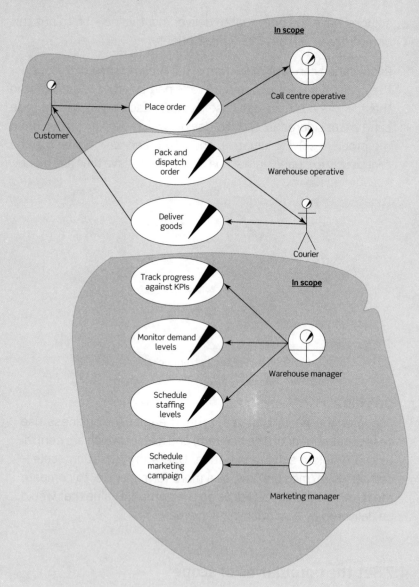

Do this

Build on the prioritisation activities described in the previous section. Use this insight to draw a boundary of scope on the business use case diagram. Meet with stakeholders to ensure there is agreement.

BIG PICTURE
4. Assessing scope and impact

4.1 The danger of 'scope creep'

Why

Having spent time articulating the nature of the *problem* (Chapter 2) and the desired *outcomes* (Chapter 3), we will now have a very precise view on the nature of the problem we are trying to solve. The trouble, though, with problems is that they don't always have rigid edges. We might find that we are solving a tricky, tangled problem and it would be very easy to start to veer off course and in doing so we might unintentionally start solving a *different* problem (leaving our original problem unsolved!).

Source: 123rf.com

Of course, if we come across different or additional problems during our problem-solving activities, it is important to consider them and decide whether we need to include them in the scope of our work. If we do, it may mean that cost, time or the amount of resource that we need is increased. However, in many cases we may decide to deliberately *exclude* other problems from our activities. They may be candidates for future or additional work, but we may choose to deliberately defer further action so that we can retain a laser-like focus on the outcomes that our stakeholders have signed up to.

To achieve this level of focus we need to avoid inadvertent 'scope creep'. It is very easy for us to unconsciously increase the scope by a feature here and an outcome there – but over time the scope of our work becomes unmanageable and we are (metaphorically) trying to 'boil the ocean'. Managing scope is crucial.

Knowledge briefing

Scope can be defined as:

> 'The boundaries of control, change, a solution or a need.'
> (International Institute of Business Analysis (IIBA), 2015)

The type of scope we are concerned with will vary throughout the problem-solving lifecycle. Initially, we will be concerned with the scope of the *problem* or *need* – this involves defining the problem, and the required outcomes. The problem statement, and the CSFs and KPIs provide a useful guiding beacon allowing us to control the scope of our activities.

As the problem-solving initiative continues, it will be necessary to agree the scope of a *change* or *solution*. In many cases, we'll be able to implement a solution that meets all of the needs and achieves all of the objectives (and we'll be able to do so within the constraints of time and budget that are put upon us). In this case, the *solution* scope is the same as the scope of *the problem*.

However, in other cases we might have less time or budget than we need to solve every aspect of the problem. In which case, *prioritisation* will be necessary. Our *solution scope*, in this case will be smaller than the scope of *the problem*. We will be solving part of the problem, often the most problematic or painful part, and leaving some elements unsolved. This may also be the case when we are delivering a solution incrementally – the highest value part of the solution will be delivered early, with additional features incremented over time.

Ensuring there is agreement over scope, and managing it carefully is crucial.

How

The very act of defining a problem statement is an excellent way of agreeing a high level problem scope. Adding a boundary of scope on the fishbone diagram also helps. Defining outcomes with CSFs and KPIs builds upon this foundation, and provides us with a useful way of defining and quantifying the outcomes that are considered most valuable. As the problem-solving activities continue, and as we start to examine potential solutions, we can ask, 'How well would that solution help us achieve those CSFs/KPIs, and how would it help us solve the problem articulated in the problem statement?' This will help keep us on scope and on track.

With this in mind, it can be extremely useful to keep the problem statement and the associated CSFs and KPIs *visible* throughout the problem-solving activities. It is worth adding these to the problem canvas early, and distributing this so that everyone relevant can see it. I often carry a copy around with me to meetings, and place it in the centre of the table. This acts as a visual cue, and often stakeholders themselves will refer to it. This subtle action helps keep us all on the same page.

Scope can be further understood and modelled with the 'roles and goals and business use case' techniques that are discussed later in this chapter. But before this, it is important to consider what and who is impacted and involved in the problem or solution – this is discussed further in the next section.

Reflection

- How did it work?

- What will I do next time?

References

International Institute of Business Analysis (IIBA), 2015. *A Guide to the Business Analysis Body of Knowledge® (BABOK® Guide)*, v3. Toronto: IIBA.

4.2 Know the difference: impacted, interested and involved

Why

When assessing and controlling the scope of a problem (and later, the solution) it is important to consider the processes, systems and stakeholders that will be directly or indirectly *impacted* as well as those that are *interested in* and those that are directly *involved* with the primary problem area. Some stakeholders may be impacted, interested *and* involved – others may fall into only one or two of these categories. This is illustrated by the diagram below – stakeholders may fall within any area of this diagram.

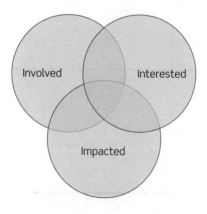

Knowledge briefing

Thinking back to our mail-order retail example that we have discussed throughout the book, our problem statement helped us conclude that a successful solution would 'ensure that we can predict and manage demand, allowing us to dispatch orders in a timely fashion, leading to increased customer satisfaction, reduced operational costs and ultimately higher profits'.

If we were to imagine the stakeholders who are likely to be directly involved in solving the problem, we might conclude that the warehouse team would be crucial. It is likely that the warehouse manager, and his team would be taking a significant interest in our problem-solving activities. We will no doubt utilise their skills and knowledge to help us form the best possible solution. They are likely to be showing a significant level of interest in our work too!

However, there may be other processes, systems and stakeholders that are *impacted* by this change. These might be equally crucial, even though the stakeholders might not be showing much or any interest at all (yet). It is key that we consider which of these need to be included in our scope. In our mail-order retailer this might include:

Area (system/ process/stakeholder)	Nature of impact
Marketing	Will potentially be a key player in helping us to 'manage demand' – potentially by varying offers to encourage orders in the quieter periods. May involve new processes/systems to support this (TBC).
Customer service	With a reduction in complaints, the team will be positively impacted. They will be able to focus on different work, and thought will need to be put into which work they should pick up (this may be outside of our scope, but somebody will need to pick it up).
Procurement	Faster dispatching may mean that there is less time available as a 'buffer' to order out-of-stock items. There may need to be re-negotiations with suppliers to ensure that any items that are out-of-stock can be delivered to the warehouse quickly. Alternatively, it may be necessary to revisit the amount of stock held.

These are just examples. The key is to consider who or what might be *impacted* – positively or negatively – when the problem is being solved and the solution is being implemented.

How

It is crucial to consider the problem from multiple perspectives and through various lenses. Ask questions like:

1. Who has an *interest* in solving this problem?

2. What other *processes, systems and people* might be impacted – either directly or indirectly?

3. Who or what sit *just outside* the boundaries of our problem scope? Might we inadvertently impact them?

4. Who will be *involved* in delivering the change and solving the problem?

5. Who will be *involved* in sustaining the change and ensuring the problem stays solved?

It is also extremely useful to examine the 'as is' situation and to utilise the 'roles and goals' technique. Both of these are discussed later in this chapter.

Reflection

- How did it work?

- What will I do next time?

```
┌─────────────────────────────────────────────────┐
│                                                   │
│                                                   │
│                                                   │
│                                                   │
│                                                   │
│                                                   │
└─────────────────────────────────────────────────┘
```

4.3 Understand the problem situation

Why

So far we have discussed defining the problem and defining outcomes. All of these things are crucial, but, by their nature tend to place more emphasis on the high-level 'bigger picture' elements of the problem. We sketch out the boundaries of the problem to ensure that there is a common view.

However, before selecting a solution it will be necessary to gain a deeper understanding of the detailed problem situation, building on the information we uncovered with our earlier fishbone diagram. It is important to understand the detailed current state, or as it is often referred to, the 'as is' situation. This involves understanding current processes, systems and organisational structures. The level of understanding that we need to gain will vary – we need to know *just enough* to ensure that any proposed solution will solve the underlying problem.

Source: Minerva Studio/Shutterstock

Knowledge briefing

There are many useful elicitation or investigation techniques that can be deployed to understand an existing situation, including those listed below:

Meetings and interviews	Whether formal or informal, it can be useful to meet with stakeholders to understand their involvement and to understand their perspective on a problem. Preparation is crucial, it is worth having a draft list of questions ready – and be prepared to deviate from these if the interviewee mentions something unexpected but relevant.
Workshops	Getting stakeholders together and holding a facilitated workshop can help us to understand the bigger picture. Workshops are often used in combination with brainstorming or other techniques to encourage input and contribution. Workshops can be a very productive forum for creating an 'as is' process model. With the right people in the room this can often be achieved quickly.
Brainstorming	Encourages divergent thinking. Start by setting a focus statement (sometimes formulated as a question, e.g. 'What are the current causes of XYZ problem?') and allow people to write their responses onto Post-it Notes. Judgement should be deferred, and the Post-it Notes can be grouped and themed later.
Observation	Seeing the problem 'first hand' is extremely valuable – this will help see the impacts and causes with our own eyes.

You will find additional resources that provide more detail about these, and other techniques, in the 'References and further reading' section.

How

1. Carry out a detailed investigation of the problem situation. The fishbone diagram produced previously will provide insight regarding *where* to look.

2. Use interviews, observation, brainstorming and workshops to delve into more detail.

3. Capture the information you gather in meeting notes, mind maps etc.

4. Consider creating models or diagrams to capture the information formally (high-level process models can be useful).

5. Validate this information with the stakeholders to ensure that there is a common and consistent understanding.

6. Avoid the temptation (yet) to talk about solutions – although if potential solution options are discussed, then capture these for later analysis and discussion.

Reflection

- How did it work?

- What will I do next time?

4.4 Find the roles and goals

Why

As discussed previously, it is important to identify stakeholders who are *impacted* by the problem, as well as stakeholders who would benefit from (or be impacted by) any solution. Understanding these stakeholders' needs will help us to craft a solution that meets their approval. If we *do not* take the time to do this, there is a risk that we might deploy a solution that meets only some of our stakeholders' needs – or even worse, it might conflict with the needs of a stakeholder group. This is likely to make us very unpopular!

To gain this understanding, it can be useful to consider the *roles* and *goals* that are involved – that is who has a particular interest, involvement or input into the problem situation (or the solution).

Source: David Lee/Shutterstock

Knowledge briefing

A *role type* represents a defined stakeholder category that have similar goals, concerns and requirements. Often this relates to their job role or functional area, although this isn't always the case. A role should be represented as a *noun*: examples include 'salesperson', 'contact centre agent' or 'customer'.

A *goal* represents an activity, process, function or feature that someone fulfilling a role would use, focussing on those that are relevant for the problem area being examined. A goal should be expressed as a *verb noun* expression. Example: 'place order', 'pay invoice' etc.

It is important to focus not just on any goals that are directly impacted by the problem, but also any that are related or indirectly impacted.

Each *role type* will have at least one goal, and each goal should be associated with at least one role type. Clearly role types can be associated with multiple goals and vice versa.

Building on the mail-order retail example we have referred to throughout the book, a first-pass of roles and goals might uncover the following:

Role type	Goal
Customer	Place order
Call centre operative	Process order
Warehouse operative	Pack and dispatch goods
Courier [external]	Deliver goods
Warehouse manager	Track progress against KPIs
Warehouse manager	Monitor demand levels
Warehouse manager	Schedule staffing levels
Marketing manager	Schedule marketing campaigns

You will notice that the number of roles that are involved is perhaps broader than we might expect. The customer has a clear interest in the problem, so it is useful at this stage to include them. Equally, we may have found that the marketing manager has an interest – perhaps she is keen to schedule marketing campaigns during quieter periods – so it would be important to ensure she is represented.

How

1. **Identify roles:** Work with your stakeholders and ask 'Who else might be involved or impacted by this problem *or* by the solution?' Ideally, write each potential role on a Post-it Note.

2. **Sort and sift roles:** Rationalise and sort the Post-it Notes (it is likely there will be duplication) and arrange them into themes. For example, you might decide that 'junior call centre operative', 'call centre worker' and 'call centre team leader' can be grouped, perhaps as 'call centre operative' – *assuming* that they all have similar goals. If you are unsure, it is best to leave them separate at this point.

3. **Identify goals:** For each role that has been identified, ask 'What is this person/group aiming to *achieve* within the context of the problem situation?' or put differently 'What are they looking to *do* – either now or once the problem has been solved?' Express these goals as a *verb noun* phrase, ideally on Post-it Notes.

4. **Sort and sift:** Sort and sift the Post-it Notes and arrange them into themes.

5. **Capture as a list:** Capture the roles and goals as a simple list, similar to the one above. This can then be presented to any stakeholders not present to seek feedback and ensure that the core goals have been captured.

Once a list of roles and goals has been created, you may choose to make it visual with a business use case diagram – this is discussed in the next section.

Reflection

- How did it work?

```



```

- What will I do next time?

```



```

4.5 Make it visual with a business use case model

Why

In the previous section we outlined how to create a list of *roles* and *goals*. Whilst this is a useful exercise in itself, a static list can be rather hard to digest – particularly when there are a large number of roles and goals. Additionally, with a static list it is difficult to show relationships between the various elements.

A business use case model is a way of visually depicting the roles and goals involved in the problem situation.

Knowledge briefing

Use cases are used in the field of business analysis to describe interactions between an 'actor' (e.g. a person or external system) and some type of 'system'. There are different types of use cases, including system use cases (which typically focus on the interaction between an actor and an IT system) and a business use case (which focusses on the valuable interactions between an actor and an organisation/business – in this case treating the *business* as a system comprising of people, processes, IT etc). In this book, we focus on *business use cases*.

This is a somewhat complex area, and in this section we cover some basics – if you find this technique useful you will find further resources in the 'References and further reading' section.

Business use case diagrams have four main symbols:

Symbol	Description	Role/Goal
	Business (external) actor: An entity *outside* of the business or organisation being analysed or discussed. This can include a person/team (role) or even an external IT system. Examples might include: customer, partner, vendor/supplier etc.	Role
	Worker (internal) actor: A role *within* the business or organisation being analysed or discussed. Examples might include: customer services, sales, manufacturing etc.	Role
	Business use case: An interaction between an actor and the business or organisation being analysed and discussed. This should be described as a short 'verb noun' phrase, describing a goal that the actor is trying to attain. Examples might include: place order, return item, query bill etc.	Goal
→	**Communication (association):** Shows which actors interact with which business use cases.	Links roles to goals

Source: These symbols are an extension to the Unified Modelling Language and are adapted from Podeswa, H., 2009. *The Business Analyst's Handbook*. Boston: Course Technology PTR, a part of Cengage Learning

A partial business use case diagram is shown below:

Here we have a business (external) actor *customer* that has the ability to initiate a business use case *place order*. This business use case also shows a supporting actor *telesales*. When the arrow representing the communication (association) points *towards* an actor, this denotes a supporting actor. A supporting actor is involved in fulfilling the business use case in some way, although they do not initiate it.

Each business use case can have multiple primary and secondary actors, as shown in the example below:

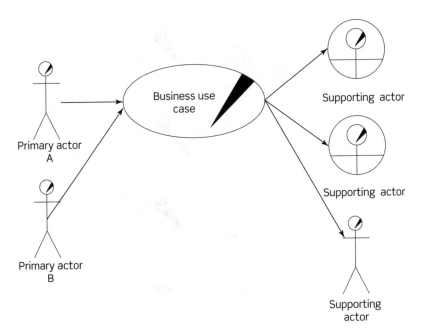

A sample business use case diagram, based on the mail-order retail case study is shown below.

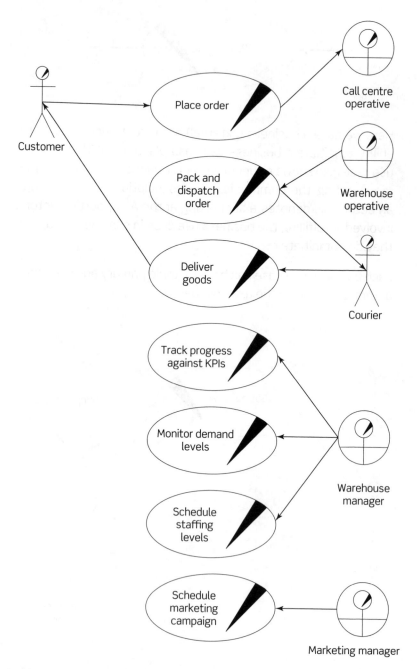

When transitioning from a list of 'roles and goals' to a business use case, it is a good opportunity to de-duplicate. For example, in the previous section we outlined goals of 'place order' for the customer and 'process order' for the call centre operative. Really these relate to the same set of activities – they are two sides of the same coin. These are represented as one single business use case 'place order', with the customer as the primary actor and the call centre operative as the supporting actor.

How

1. Work through the roles and goals list that you created earlier.

2. Identify the business (external) actors and the worker (internal) actors. Draw these on the diagram.

3. Identify the use cases. Articulate these as 'verb noun' phrases and draw them on the diagram.

4. Represent communication (associations) on the diagram, remembering to consider primary and secondary actors.

5. Review and iterate.

Reflection

- How did it work?

- What will I do next time?

```

```

References

Podeswa, H., 2009. *The Business Analyst's Handbook,* Boston: Course Technology PTR, a part of Cengage Learning.

4.6 Set the priorities

Why

Unless we are very lucky, we are almost certainly going to have constraints of time and budget pressing down on our problem-solving initiatives. Whilst it would be wonderful to solve *every* facet of *every* element of the problem, this might not be possible. Alternatively, we might need to solve the most urgent elements of the problem first, leaving some of the lower-priority aspects to wait.

In order to do this, it is important to *prioritise*.

Source: Mauro Saivezzo/Shutterstock

Knowledge briefing

Prioritisation can take many forms. In the context of our problem-solving activities, we might choose to:

- Prioritise the *outcomes* – which of the KPIs and CSFs are *most* important?

- Prioritise the *goals* – which of the *goals* (or business use cases) are highest priority for our problem-solving activity?

In many cases, the CSFs and KPIs will be difficult to prioritise. If we have elicited and analysed them well, we will have a handful of 'core' measures that really are crucial. Therefore it is often useful to focus on prioritising the *goals*.

This activity can be driven from the business use case diagram.

How

1. Consider each business use case in turn. Ask questions like 'What is the value in including this business use case in our problem-solving activity?' and 'Could any changes to this business use case wait, or are they essential?'

2. Assess the types of benefits that would be achieved by including each business use case and ensure they link to the CSFs and KPIs. If they don't, then perhaps these activities should be considered out of scope.

3. Assign each business use case a priority level. There are many prioritisation mechanisms – a simple numeric scale, or perhaps a scale of 'high, medium, low' can be used, or more formal mechanisms like MoSCoW can be used. Alternatively, a simple scale of 'mandatory' and 'desirable' can be used.

(For an explanation of the MoSCoW technique see Cadle, Paul and Turner (2014).)

Reflection

- How did it work?

- What will I do next time?

References

Cadle, J., Paul, D. and Turner, P., 2014. *Business Analysis Techniques: 99 Essential Techniques for Success*. Swindon: BCS.

4.7 Set the boundaries of scope

Why

Previously in this chapter, we discussed the importance of avoiding 'scope creep'. One way of doing this is to ensure that our scope is clearly articulated. Our problem statement and our CSFs and KPIs provide an excellent starting point, but this can be built upon by utilising our business use case diagram. Annotating the *scope* on our business use case diagram is easy to do, and will help avoid future conflict, disagreement and general wrangling over scope.

Knowledge briefing

Once prioritisation has taken place, a discussion can be held around *which* business use cases should continue to form part of our problem-solving activity. This can be made visual by drawing a boundary of scope on the business use case diagram, as illustrated in the example below:

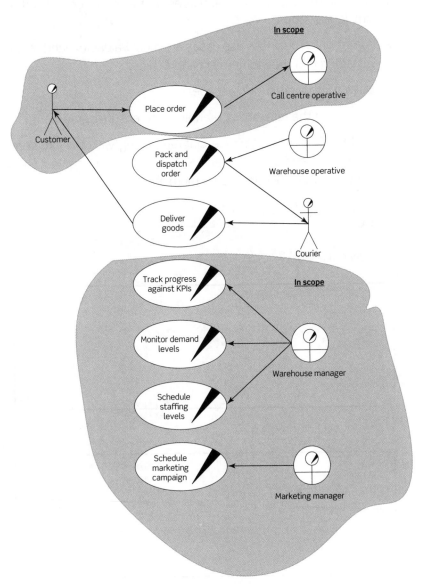

This diagram clearly shows the business use cases that are in and out of scope, and used correctly will leave no room for ambiguity or misunderstanding.

How

1. Build on the prioritisation activities that were described in the previous section.

2. Agree which business use cases are most valuable/need to be considered in the problem-solving activity.

3. Draw a line representing scope.

4. Meet with the relevant stakeholders to ensure agreement.

5. Add the business use case diagram, along with the problem statement and the CSFs and KPIs to a problem canvas (see Section 1.7 and Section 6.1 for more about the problem canvas).

Reflection

- How did it work?

- What will I do next time?

Chapter 5

Solutioneering: generating solution options

5.1 Keep the outcomes clearly in mind

So far in this book, we have mainly focussed on defining and understanding the *problem*. In this chapter, we examine how to consider potential *solutions*, and how to narrow down those potential solutions to a manageable number.

As we start to think about solutions, it is important that we steer away from the temptation to settle on the first solution that seems viable. In most situations it is valuable to think divergently, and generate a number of competing solution options – rather than settling on the first that we happen to stumble upon. By thinking broader we may come across an option that is cheaper, better and quicker than we envisaged. Thinking broader also helps us avoid 'knee-jerk' reactions to problems, which may not have been well thought through.

Keeping the desired outcomes clearly in mind helps us steer away from these problems.

Source: Lightspring/Shutterstock

Do this

Create a partially completed problem canvas (see Chapter 6), with the problem statement, business use case diagram and CSFs/KPIs clearly stated. Bring this to meetings and use it to guide further conversations and steer these discussions away from a sub-conscious knee-jerk solution focus. Relate conversations to the outcomes, to ensure that they are front-of-mind.

5.2 Get together and imagine multiple solutions

An important first step towards choosing a solution is to create an unstructured list of *potential* solutions. This may be created through a combination of desk-based research, interviews and also brainstorming. Often useful insight comes from getting people together and brainstorming. This allows people to build on each other's ideas and create new or additional options that may not have emerged if we relied purely on interviews and research.

This initial list of potential solutions can be very long indeed – the initial aim is to focus on *quantity* over *quality*. In Section 5.3 and Section 5.4 we will discuss refining the list further. Therefore, it is important to brief the participants at the beginning of the workshop and set a clear expectation of the purpose of the session.

Source: nasirkhan/Shutterstock

Do this

Convene a workshop and ensure that the participants have a clear expectation of the purpose of the session. Keep the CSFs, KPIs and problem statement clearly visible during the session, and set a clear focus statement so that the team know the problem they are aiming to solve.

5.3 Start evaluating solutions: create a 'long list'

The brainstorming activities mentioned in the previous section will generate a large quantity of ideas – but only some of these will be feasible given the constraints of the project. Some might be clearly too expensive, time consuming, risky or outlandish. This is also an opportunity to remove or combine any duplicate suggestions that have been raised. There may even be some ideas suggested that don't fully solve the problem (or some that aren't a good fit within the organisation). The next logical stage is to 'weed out' any outliers so that we are left with a long list of possible solutions that – at a first pass – seem feasible. These can be taken forward for further analysis.

This initial evaluation process is best conducted soon after the initial brainstorming session, and the group that helped to generate the ideas are often well placed to help evaluate which of the ideas are most feasible too. Comparing each suggestion/potential solution in turn, the group will consider the feasibility and the extent that it will meet the overall objectives (and any other relevant factors). By the end of the session, an agreed 'long list' will be carried forward.

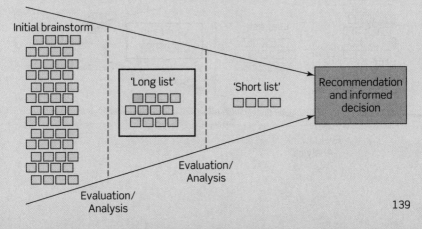

Initial brainstorm

'Long list'

'Short list'

Recommendation and informed decision

Evaluation/Analysis

Evaluation/Analysis

Evaluation/Analysis

Do this

As soon as possible after the brainstorming activity, work to rationalise the list of ideas generated to create a long list. Work with the group to establish which of the ideas will meet the objectives that are encapsulated in the CSFs and KPIs, which are within scope, and which have the highest possible chance of success.

5.4 Getting specific: short list the best

In the previous section, we discussed creating a 'long list'. The next step is for us to prune the list down to, perhaps, three or four options that are most likely to be viable. In order to do this, work each solution up into a short description – just a few paragraphs – and consider how the solution would work. Also consider the likely benefits, costs and risks. This may require further high-level analysis – perhaps speaking with solution providers or vendors (to get an idea of likely areas of cost) – but it should be noted that this is very much an initial 'gut feel'. It is designed to allow comparison between options, rather than needing to ascribe a finite figure to the costs or benefits.

The short-listed options will be carried forward, where a more thorough analysis of costs, benefits and other relevant factors can take place where appropriate.

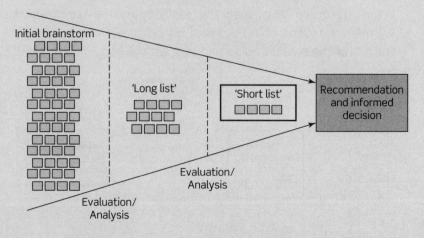

Do this

Use the template provided in the 'Big picture' section of this chapter (Section 5.4) to compare each long-listed option. Remember that this is intended as a relatively quick exercise, and whilst it may be necessary to carry out some further high-level analysis/investigation, we only need enough information to *compare* the options.

5.5 Consider doing nothing

When creating a short list, an option that we should consider is *doing nothing*. This creates a useful baseline, and helps us compare the relative merits of doing *something*. It helps us ensure we do not inadvertently assume that we *have* to take action when actually doing nothing might (sometimes) be a viable option of its own.

Doing nothing involves assessing what will happen if the problem *isn't* solved. What will happen to costs? Revenue? What will get worse? What will stay the same? What are the impacts (both positive and negative)?

Source: Dimec/Shutterstock

Do this

Use the template provided in Section 5.4 to examine the 'do nothing' option. Compare and contrast this against the other options that are being considered.

5.6 Compare the short-listed options

Having created a short list of three or four options, the next step is for us to compare them against each other. This will involve understanding more about the pros and cons of each solution, so that an objective recommendation can be made over which solution to adopt. As a minimum, it is useful to consider the costs, benefits and risks of each option. It will be necessary to engage with relevant experts or solution providers (e.g. vendors) to understand or estimate the costs, and a different set of experts will help us to understand the likely benefits.

The size and formality of the problem-solving initiative will determine the level of analysis that takes place. For very small incremental changes, a cursory estimate of costs may suffice. When implementing a multi-million pound IT system, it's likely that a formal business case will be required. It's important to understand your organisation's project governance process, as this may impose particular steps or templates.

Source: Roobcio/Shutterstock

Do this

Establish the detailed pros and cons of each of the short-listed options, paying particular attention to costs, benefits and risks. Remember that benefits and costs can be intangible as well as tangible. Ensure that you adhere to any internal project governance steps.

5.7 Validate and make a recommendation

Having compared each short-listed solution, we are now ready to make a recommendation. Making a recommendation is a careful balancing act. Clearly we need to consider the benefits, costs, risks and so forth – but we also need to be as sure as we can be that the solution *will* solve the problem and also that it will fit within any constraints (time/budget). We may find that the external business environment makes some solutions more favourable than others, so we would be well advised to revisit our STEEPLE analysis.

How we assess and make our recommendation will depend on the formality that is required. For large scale changes or where a high level of formality is needed, we may choose to use a formal scoring mechanism; for smaller or less formal changes a qualitative list of pros and cons may suffice. Either way, we need to provide the decision maker with sufficient information to confidently make a decision.

Source: Veerachai Viteeman/Shutterstock

Do this
Build on the list of pros and cons, considering wider aspects of the problem and the business environment. Compare the options, and provide a clear recommendation. State any assumptions made so the decision maker is completely clear on the decision they are making.

BIG PICTURE
5. Solutioneering: generating solution options

5.1 Keep the outcomes clearly in mind

Why

So far, we have discussed ways of defining the *problem* we are trying to solve and the *outcomes* that we need to achieve. The next logical step is to consider potential solutions. However, experience tells us that the human brain has a tendency to make 'snap judgements' – and left unchecked these can lead to knee-jerk decisions of the type we discussed earlier. Often a specific solution might hold a special allure; perhaps there's a new software package that is '*en vogue*' and our stakeholders feel that it is *crucial* that we buy it. Of course, the software *might* be the best option – but until we've examined and considered a range of options this will be extremely uncertain. Furthermore, if we buy the software and find out that it *doesn't* solve our problem, then we have probably just made a very expensive mistake!

Our problem-solving activity so far has helped us avoid these kind of knee-jerk activities – keeping the outcomes in mind throughout whilst we consider solutions (a process sometimes known as 'solutioneering') is crucial.

Source: LightSpring/Shutterstock

Knowledge briefing

In the well-respected book *Thinking, Fast and Slow,* Nobel Prize Winner Daniel Kahneman outlines two types of thinking:

System 1 Thinking: Enables us to make quick, intuitive assessments and decisions. System 1 thinking is unconscious, and built upon our experiences and prejudices. System 1 enables you to hit the brakes on a car when a pedestrian steps out – an activity that you haven't had to consciously think about. System 1 reacts in a general way and so can give misleading responses (I was once bitten by a dog as a child; a traumatic event. I still have an irrational fear of certain types of dog, and I have to 'override' my brain's instinctive desire to stay away from them).

System 2 Thinking: Enables us to carry out detailed analysis and calculations. Answering the question "What is 233 x 14" would engage System 2.

(Adapted from Kahneman, 2012)

Often, we may come up with a 'gut feel' over what the best solution is. We shouldn't disregard this, but it is worth encouraging *divergent thinking* – there may be many other solutions too. And our 'gut feel' (and System 1 Thinking) may have led us to *assume* a certain solution will work, when perhaps this is not the case.

How

1. **Keep outcomes visible:** Ensure that the desired *outcomes* are displayed clearly during solutioneering activities. Consider creating a partially completed problem canvas and bringing this to meetings. It is useful to place it in the centre of the table, or somewhere equally visible. (See Section 1.7 and Section 6.1 for more about the problem canvas.)

2. **Encourage divergent thinking first:** Throughout the early stages of our solutioneering activity it is valuable to encourage divergent thinking, to ensure a range of ideas are tabled. Using the diagram included in Section 2.3 can help ensure a

common understanding and help to set expectations with our stakeholders.

Reflection

- How did it work?

(blank box)

- What will I do next time?

(blank box)

References

Kahneman, D., 2012. *Thinking, Fast and Slow*. London: Penguin.

5.2 Get together and imagine multiple solutions

Why

As alluded to in the previous section, it is beneficial to avoid jumping on the first solution we find. In many cases, there will be a whole multitude of potential solution options available to us. It is useful – both individually, and in groups – to imagine potential types of solution that can be explored.

Source: Palto/Shutterstock

Knowledge briefing

A logical starting point is to identify broad types of solution options available to us. These might start as broad as 'Buy a CRM software package' or they may be more specific, for example 'Improve the sales process so that payment is taken earlier'. Either way, these solution options are still high level, and further analysis and detail would be required.

There are a number of ways that we might uncover different solution options. Benchmarking and research can provide further insight ('How have others solved this problem?' and 'What do our competitors do?'). White papers and research from consultancies can provide further information too. Although it should be noted that simply *copying* other organisations, whilst it might bring you on par with your competitors, is unlikely (on its own) to drive competitive advantage.

Additionally, our stakeholders are a rich source of potential solution options. It can be valuable to convene a brainstorming workshop and encourage the attendees to come up with as many options as possible. Initial brainstorming is very much about *quantity* – it may be that some ideas are not feasible, but the very act of producing them allows us to consider them. We may also find that the best option is to *combine* several ideas – perhaps each idea was infeasible in isolation, but when combined they produce the perfect outcome.

How

1. Convene a workshop. Set the scene, and encourage the attendees to generate as many ideas as possible. Instil a collaborative environment by setting some 'brainstorming rules', which might include:

   - Defer judgement: worry about feasibility later.
   - Go for quantity: don't self-censor. Anything goes.
   - All ideas are equal: irrespective of the seniority of the person who raised them.

2. Have the desired outcomes on display: make the problem statement, CSFs and KPIs visible. They don't need to constrain our thinking, but they do need to act as a guiding beacon representing our aims.

3. Set a clear focus statement for the brainstorming activity: this could be as simple as 'How do we solve the problem of X?', or you may choose to use more elaborate focus statements.

4. Encourage people to contribute as many ideas as possible.

5. After the brainstorming activity has finished, work with the group to sort, sift, de-duplicate and group the ideas into themes for later discussion.

Reflection

- How did it work?

- What will I do next time?

5.3 Start evaluating solutions: create a 'long list'

Why

In the previous section, we discussed brainstorming and identifying potential solution options. During this initial brainstorm, the focus will be on creating as many ideas as possible, without worrying (yet) about how feasible they are.

Having encouraged this kind of *divergent thinking*, it is important that we move on to *converge* on a set of solutions that are most appropriate. This starts by 'weeding out' any solutions that are clearly inappropriate/unachievable, and by prioritising those that are most likely to be desirable and feasible. This activity will create an initial 'long list' of solutions that can be assessed in more detail.

Knowledge briefing

Brainstorming will often generate hundreds of potential ideas, but in the cold light of day only some of these are likely to be feasible and desirable. We could carry out a full analysis of every single idea, but this will take significant time and resources – therefore a three-stage approach is useful: firstly, creating a large number of options through an initial brainstorm, then evaluating these quickly and creating a 'long list'. Then, a further evaluation and comparison can take place to create a 'short list'.

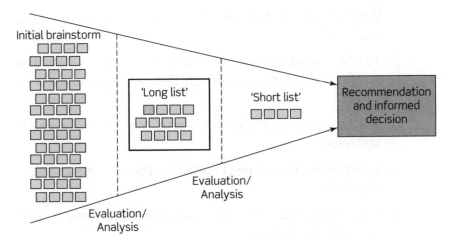

In this section we will discuss creating the 'long list'.

This initial stage of evaluation and analysis allows us to cast aside any ideas that are definitely not achievable, for whatever reason, as well as those that don't actually *solve* the problem we are looking to address. It acts as our first 'filter', allowing us to focus on the solutions that are most likely to be feasible and valuable. In doing so, we are comparing, contrasting and *converging* on likely solutions.

How

This initial evaluation activity can be carried out immediately after *generating* the ideas, and works well when carried out in a workshop environment. However, it is useful to have a short coffee break between the idea generation and evaluation sections of a workshop, to allow people time to 'reset' and reflect.

When preparing for this activity, it is worth having the problem statement, CSFs, KPIs and business use case diagram visible. Work with the group and take each idea/theme that has been generated in turn. Ask questions like:

1. Will this meet the objectives that are encapsulated in the CSFs and KPIs?

2. To what extent will it meet the objectives? (Priority should be given to those that meet the objectives entirely, or to a greater extent.)

3. Will this address the problem articulated in the problem statement?

4. Is this within the scope indicated on the business use case diagram?

5. Is this achievable within any known constraints (time, budget, resource, technical etc)?

6. Is this solution an appropriate cultural fit for our organisation?

7. Could this idea be combined or merged with another to create a more effective option?

This activity can often be undertaken relatively quickly. If each idea/theme has been written on a Post-it Note, it can be useful to create three piles: *Yes, No* and *Don't Know (Defer)*. Any ideas that feel like a good fit, that should certainly move forward to the next stage of evaluation go in the *Yes* pile, any clear outliers that should not move forward into the *No*, any where further information is required (so an immediate decision cannot be made) are moved into the *Don't Know (Defer)* pile. This prevents conversation centring on these – against each of these items, record the information that is needed, and then seek this soon after the meeting. This is illustrated on the diagram that follows below.

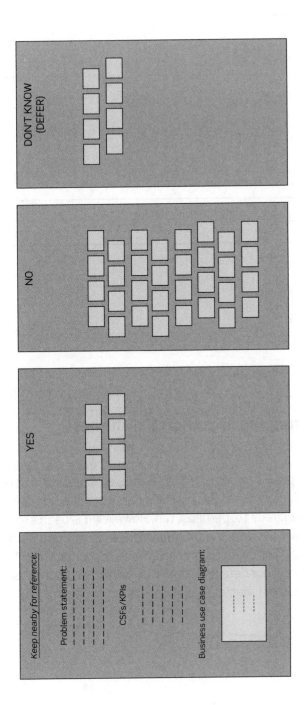

Reflection

- How did it work?

- What will I do next time?

5.4 Getting specific: short list the best

Why

In the previous section we discussed creating a *long list* of potential solutions. This will have pared our solution options down from hundreds to, perhaps, ten. However, it is useful to prune the list down even further. In many cases it will be appropriate to prune the list down to, perhaps, three or four options. This allows us to focus our detailed efforts on just those three or four options that are most viable.

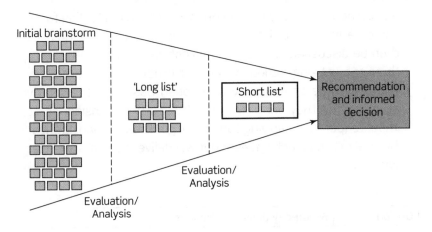

Knowledge briefing

Short listing requires a more detailed analysis of each option to take place, however this analysis is kept at a fairly high level. When creating a long list, the questions we ask will tend to be fairly abstract ('Could a new computer package help solve this problem?'), when short listing we move to a lower level of abstraction and start to discuss some of the concrete details ('Is there a suitable computer package available, and are we likely to have the resources to deploy it?').

This may require us to carry out research or even contact vendors/ suppliers of particular solutions to request general information. We may also need to consult with wider stakeholders in our organisation to understand the impact of particular options.

How

Take each of the long-listed ideas and work it up into a short description – a few paragraphs – which describes more about *how* the solution would work and the benefits it would achieve. Taking our mail-order retailer, one potential solution option could be offering a discount for seven-day delivery.

It would be useful to work this up into a wider solution description, linking back to the problem statement, and outlining the main areas of impact, cost and benefit (see table below).

As outlined above, it can be useful to get an initial feeling for the comparative level of benefit, cost and impact. These ideas can then be discussed and ranked against each other, with the top three or four being carried forward to the next stage of evaluation. The top three or four may be chosen based on the relative benefits that they bring, *or* it may be useful to consider costs/impacts (perhaps carrying forward a 'gold', 'silver' and 'bronze' – 'bronze' may be much cheaper but will deliver comparatively less benefit).

Option	Seven-day delivery discount
Description	
Offering a discount for a seven-day delivery will enable us to better manage demand. We anticipate, based on knowledge of our customer base, that around 40–60 per cent of customers would choose this option. We will save money by utilising discount couriers, and if times are busy, we'll have up to six days to pack and dispatch the order.	
Impacted areas	
This will require changes to the order process, a minor tweak to the order database, a change to the dispatch process and will require a training and communication plan.	
Main benefits	
Will enable us to manage demand – we can avoid 'spikes' and the warehouse team will be able to rely less on overtime and temporary workers (reducing the wages bill). We also provide another delivery option for our customers, increasing satisfaction. We can utilise discount couriers, reducing costs.	
Main costs	
Analysis and rolling out of changed order process. Specification and implementation of a tweak to the order database. Costs have not yet been estimated in financial terms.	
Main risks	
Risk that customers may not adopt/use this delivery option to the extent that we expect them to.	
Comments	
This solution option is comparatively low impact, and low cost, and will deliver a medium benefit. If it were to be considered viable, a more detailed estimate will be produced.	

Version control							
Author	SD	Updated	4 Feb	Status	Draft	Version	0.1

Reflection

- How did it work?

- What will I do next time?

5.5 Consider doing nothing

Why

As counterintuitive as it may sound, once we start evaluating potential solution options, it is also useful to consider what would happen if we *do nothing*. Or, to put this in a different way, what if we *don't* solve the problem?

This is an important consideration as it helps us obtain a *baseline* – it may be, for example, in our mail-order retail example that if we do nothing that we anticipate complaints rise and profits reduce. This will help make a compelling case for doing *something*! Of course, in other situations, doing nothing might be the most viable option – and carrying out this analysis may have saved us making a knee-jerk decision that would cost money and deliver little or no benefit.

Source: Sergii Korolko/Shutterstock

Knowledge briefing

It is important to consider the impact of doing nothing. This requires us to hypothesise or predict what might happen if the problem is not addressed. It is worthwhile quantifying this in financial terms, whilst also considering intangible factors and risk too. The aim is to create an objective and concise picture of what is likely to happen if the current state remains unchanged.

Useful questions include:

- Is the problem likely to get worse over time, or will it stay the same?
- If it will get worse, to what extent and how quickly?
- What would happen to our customer base if the problem is left unsold?
- Will there be any impact on top-line revenue?
- Will there be any impact on costs?
- Are there any legal or regulatory impacts?
- What are the impacts on our staff?
- Are there any other stakeholders who would continue to be affected, if so what impact would this cause?
- Might there be any reputational impacts?
- Are there any other possible tangible or intangible impacts? How likely are they?
- Are there any critical deadline dates, if so what are they (and why)?

How

1. Start with a brief description of the impact of doing nothing.

2. Use the headings in the table in Section 5.4 and the questions above as a starting point to further examine/elaborate the option.

3. Work with a small group of relevant stakeholders to thoroughly understand the option.

4. Pay particular attention to risks.

5. For each potential risk event, also list the consequences of that risk, and whether there are any ways the risk can be avoided, mitigated or transferred.

6. Remember, at this stage we are looking for a concise *summary* of each option – further analysis will follow – so focus on the most significant facets for now.

Reflection

- How did it work?

- What will I do next time?

5.6 Compare the short-listed options

Why

Having created a short list of, say, three potential solutions allows us to directly compare and contrast them. With a manageable number of solutions, we can collect and collate data so that an objective decision can be made. Depending on the nature and size of the problem, we may put together a formal 'business case' style document – or for less formal/smaller problems, we may just summarise the key benefits and costs of each option. If your organisation has a specific project governance process, it is important to ensure that this is taken into account as it may mean there are specific templates or steps that are required before a decision on solution can be made or before spend can be committed to.

Source: Nelson Marques/Shutterstock

Knowledge briefing

In order to objectively evaluate different solutions, as a minimum, it is useful to know and consider the factors shown in the table below.

There are more sophisticated ways of evaluating the costs/benefits of different options, which are beyond the scope of this book. There are resources mentioned in the 'References and further reading' section that will be of interest to readers who are putting together a formal business case.

Factor	Description	Example
Cost of implementation	Costs associated with making the change	£x to purchase a new database server
Cost of running/ maintaining solution	Ongoing costs that must be paid on a regular basis	£x annual licensing of software £y staff costs
Benefits, tangible and financial	Benefits that can be predicted with a reasonable level of certainty and quantified in financial terms	£x saving in courier costs £y reduction in licensing costs
Benefits, tangible but not financial	Benefits that can be predicted with a reasonable level of certainty and quantified in non-financial terms	A reduction in processing time from 20 minutes to 10 minutes
Benefits, intangible	Benefits that cannot be predicted and quantified in advance with any level of accuracy	Increased brand awareness Increased customer satisfaction
Costs, intangible	Costs that cannot be predicted and quantified in advance with any level of confidence	Productivity will temporarily drop whilst people get used to the new process
Risks	Uncertain events that may affect the organisation or the change. It is also valuable to capture any risk avoidance, mitigation or transference options available	Our customers may not adopt the new process and may instead choose to buy from a competitor, leading to lost revenue and reduced profit

How

Work with the stakeholders and solution providers/vendors to establish ballpark cost and benefit estimates for each of the short-listed options. Compare each option – ideally we are looking for the option that offers the highest recurring benefits for the lowest costs and lowest risks. However, producing a recommendation often involves carefully weighing up the pros and cons – this is discussed in the next section.

Reflection

- How did it work?

- What will I do next time?

5.7 Validate and make a recommendation

Why

We have reached a crucial part of the problem-solving lifecycle. We have examined several solutions, and are ready to make a recommendation. The recommendation will clearly signpost the best solution (or solutions), and will state the next actions that need to be taken.

Source: JohnKwan/Shutterstock

Artefact/Consideration	See Section	Considerations/Questions to ask
Costs and benefits	5.6	What level of budget is available? Which solution offers the best return on investment for the budget available? How does the organisation measure financial success?
Problem statement	2.2	Does each solution solve the *whole* problem? Does one solution solve it in a comparatively better or more comprehensive way?
Outcomes: balanced scorecard (CSFs and KPIs)	3.2 3.3 3.4	Which solution best meets the CSFs and KPIs?
Scope: business use case diagram	4.4 4.5 4.6	Which solution best fits within the defined scope?
As is	2.4 4.3	Which solution is most compatible with the existing ('as is') situation? If change is necessary, is there appetite to implement that change?
Risks	6.6	What is the risk appetite of the organisation? Are any solutions too risky? Is the organisation prepared to accept more risk for a greater return?
Constraints	1.6 3.5	Which solution best meets any constraints (time, budget, quality, technical etc)?
External environment: STEEPLE	2.5	Which solution is best aligned with the organisation's external business environment? Which is more likely to be 'future proof'?

Knowledge briefing

Making a recommendation is a careful balancing act. Often we are comparing very different solutions, each of which has different benefits, costs and risks associated. It is useful to validate and map each potential solution back to the problem statement, outcome and scope that we defined earlier.

It is also crucial to understand and revisit any constraints, including budget or time, so that we can ensure the recommendation will be achievable within them.

How

Arriving at a recommendation involves weighing up the solutions against the priorities of the organisation and its stakeholders. It is important to work out with stakeholders *how to decide*. The decision process for a small problem-solving initiative (e.g. speeding up a step in a process) is likely to be far less formal than that of a large multi-million initiative (e.g. increase profit by launching a new product in a new market).

Where a *formal and objective* decision-making process is required, it can be useful to create a scoring and weighting mechanism. The relative costs and benefits can be ranked, based on criteria that are important to the organisation and its stakeholders. The categories in the table above can be built upon, with evaluation criteria added to each of them. The evaluation criteria should be made as objective and specific as possible. Formal investment appraisal techniques including payback period, discounted cash flow/net present value and Internal Rate of Return (IRR) can help to make informed and objective decisions on the financial elements – readers interested in these techniques will find useful resources in the 'References and further reading' section.

Where a *less formal* decision-making process is required, it may be sufficient to compile a qualitative list of pros and cons and to discuss this with the relevant stakeholders. It is still important to ensure objectivity, and we must be on guard to unconsciously prevent any bias affecting the decision.

Either way, we should produce a recommendation and then consider the next steps to get our change implemented. Once we have a clear recommendation, we can bring our problem-solving activities together into a single concise and precise problem-solving canvas. This is discussed in the next chapter.

Reflection

- How did it work?

- What will I do next time?

Chapter 6

Bringing it all together: the one-page 'problem canvas'

6. Bringing it all together: the one-page 'problem canvas'

6.1 Being concise and precise: building the canvas

A problem canvas is a single-page template that concisely summarises the problem that we are trying to solve, the scope, along with the solutions that we are considering (and the recommended next actions). It brings together all of the previous work onto a single sheet so that we can ensure that everyone is literally 'on the same page'. As outlined in Chapter 1, it articulates a thin-slice of the 'why', the 'what' and the 'how' of the problem-solving initiative.

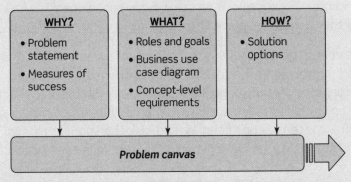

Source: Blackmetric Business Soluctions

It is good practice to build the problem canvas iteratively as our initial problem analysis activities take place, and indeed we have referred to this several times during the book. However, once we have carried out all of the activities described in Chapters 1–5, we will be well placed to ensure that every section of the canvas is completed. Once completed, we can ensure that the various areas of the canvas are consistent, and that key stakeholders agree – gaining consensus is discussed in the next section. Once agreed, the canvas becomes a useful guiding beacon for future work.

An example problem canvas is included in the 'Big picture' section of this chapter (Section 6.1).

Do this

Having built up the problem canvas iteratively throughout the problem and solution analysis process, take one last opportunity to fill in any blanks and check for completeness. This ensures it is ready for a final review with the key stakeholders.

6.2 Gaining consensus

Having put a complete version of the problem canvas together, it is time to review it with the relevant stakeholders. It is useful to bring people together, and reflect on (and review) each section. You will have been doing this iteratively, however this additional review provides the opportunity to take a look at the canvas as a whole – holistically – and carry out a 'sense check' before any further work takes place.

In order to gain consensus, it is important to consider *who* needs to be involved in the review. Contact the relevant people, and arrange a workshop or review session. Walk through each section in turn, making any necessary amendments where necessary. Once consensus has been agreed, ask the sponsor to 'sign off' and store it in a central location where everyone can have access.

Source: Zphoto/Shutterstock

Do this
Get the relevant people together to review the problem canvas, and once it is agreed, store it in a centrally accessible location so it can be a guiding beacon for future work.

6.3 The canvas as an internal sales tool

To ensure that our problem-solving initiative works as efficiently as possible, we may need to 'sell' the benefits to groups or individuals. There may be stakeholder groups – inside or outside of our organisation – who aren't directly involved in the initiative, but are crucial to its success. We may need to influence them even though we have no authority.

The problem canvas can be an extremely useful sales tool. It succinctly summarises the *need* for change, the *scope* of change and the *benefits*. When explaining the initiative to customers, suppliers, partners, end-users and front line staff, we may drive a conversation *from* the canvas. We can leave a copy of the canvas with them so that they can pass the information on to their team mates and staff. This is an opportunity for us to build rapport, to communicate and to hear any concerns that people may have.

Source: StockLite/Shutterstock

Do this

Use the problem canvas as a tool for communicating the *need* for change, the *scope* of the change and the *benefits*. Use it to bring people on-board, and where possible ensure they are supportive and enthusiastic about the change. Where people are not immediately supportive, use it as a tool to help them pinpoint their concerns.

6.4 Gain commitment

Solving a problem is a group effort. Whilst we might be co-ordinating it ourselves, we might need actions and input from a range of colleagues – potentially inside and outside of our organisation. This input might be needed during the analysis phase, when building the canvas – and is likely to ramp up significantly once a solution is chosen. It is crucial that we *ask* people for their commitment and for their time. There is no point embarking on a problem-solving initiative if the right people are not behind it and willing and able to help. If they don't have the time, then perhaps it would be better to defer the initiative to a time when they do (or to plan or schedule the initiative differently, or to try to solve the problem in a different way).

Source: Michael D. Brown/Shutterstock

Do this
Ask for people's commitment on particular tasks. Build a Responsible, Accountable, Consulted, Informed (RACI) matrix to clearly articulate who is *responsible* and/or *accountable* for each task, and who needs to be *consulted* and/or *informed*.

6.5 Plan the next steps

To ensure that action actually *happens* it is necessary to create a plan. This involves understanding the tasks, the effort/duration, the dependencies, and the people required to do them. Ideally, on large scale initiatives, a project manager would be assigned to undertake this planning – but if no project manager is assigned, we might need to find somebody else to undertake this planning in the short term (or we may need to do elements of it ourselves).

The schedule should clearly show the timeline, tasks and deliverables/milestones, and should be *communicated* so that everyone knows what should happen when. It can then be used to track progress.

Source: ALMAGAMI/Shutterstock

Do this
Work with a project manager to create a project schedule – perhaps as a Gantt chart. Ensure the tasks, deliverables, milestones and dependencies between tasks are shown.

6.6 Beware risks

Problem solving inherently carries risks. If we are implementing new solutions, there may be uncertainties and predictable problems that *might* happen that we can plan for. A risk can be defined as:

> *'The effect of uncertainty on the value of a change, a solution, or the enterprise.'*
>
> (International Institute of Business Analysis (IIBA), 2015)

When we are pushing forward with our problem-solving initiative it is useful to consider in detail what risks are relevant for the particular chosen solution. Ask questions like 'What might stop us?' and 'What might cause us to veer off track?' Having identified risks, we can consider what risk modification action to take – for example finding ways to *avoid* the risk, *mitigate* it, *transfer* it or *accept* it.

Source: Gunnar Pippel/Shutterstock

Do this

Work with your team to create a risk log. If you have assigned a project manager, ensure that you work with them and the project team to capture risks and identify risk modification activities. Ensure the risk log is regularly revisited and that each risk has an 'owner' who is responsible for specific identified actions.

6.7 A problem canvas is a great place to start (but the hard work is yet to come)

A problem canvas is a useful artefact to help us quickly define a problem, desired outcomes and possible solutions. However, it's important to know when the canvas is *good enough* for us to get going and actually *implement* (or plan the implementation of) a solution. It could be tempting to spend hours (or days) 'polishing' the canvas – but the intention is always for the canvas to be a quick, light-weight, concise yet precise document. It should *enable* action rather than *prevent* it.

Work with stakeholders to assess the relative size and cost of the problem, the volume of benefits that may be realised by solving it, and the size, cost and nature of the problem. For small solutions that require just a few hours work to implement, the canvas may provide sufficient detail to 'hit the ground running'. Larger projects may need further clarification and more detailed requirements. Either way, it is important to note that whilst the canvas helps us consider the problem and define a solution, by itself it does not *implement* the solution! Further hard work is yet to come, and it is important that we ensure that everyone is willing and able to take the next steps.

Source: John Foxx Collection/Imagestate

Do this

Consider the size and impact of the problem and solution to determine whether the canvas provides enough information to 'hit the ground running', or whether a more formal feasibility phase is required. For anything but the smallest of initiatives, it is likely that further work will be needed – ensure people are aware and bought into this.

BIG PICTURE

6. Bringing it all together: the one-page 'problem canvas'

6.1 Being concise and precise: building the canvas

Why

The problem canvas is an extremely useful artefact that concisely and precisely summarises the problem we are trying to solve, the outcomes we are looking to achieve, the scope *and* the solutions that we are considering. It brings together all of the work that we have done onto a single page.

It is normal to build this up iteratively – it will start blank, and different elements will be added once we have created them.

Once the problem canvas is complete, it provides a guiding beacon for our future work. It ensures that everyone will stay focussed on the problem in hand, and helps us avoid the slippery slope of scope creep.

Knowledge briefing

An example problem canvas for our mail-order retailer example is shown below. The problem canvas has several key sections:

- **Problem name and version control:** The first few sections relate to the problem canvas itself:
  - Problem name: A short 'nickname' for the problem. It is good practice to assign each problem a unique name, so that when we are in conversation with our stakeholders, we can be sure we are talking about the same problem!

- Canvas ID: A unique reference number – this is important in large enterprises where tens (or hundreds) of problem-solving initiatives may be happening in parallel.
- Portfolio: If the problem-solving activity falls within a larger portfolio of work, this portfolio can be mentioned here.
- Sponsor: The person who is *sponsoring* the problem-solving activity. This is the person ultimately accountable for the activity, and the person who is providing the budget.
- Canvas author: The person who created the canvas.
- Canvas version: A version number. Assigning a version number is useful, as we can be sure that we are all looking at the correct version (e.g. 'Do we all have version 1.2 in front of us?').
- Date: The date the canvas was last updated.
- Status: The status of the canvas. Possible status types might include 'draft', 'under review', 'signed off' etc.
- Confidence: The confidence that the *canvas author* has that the information shown is accurate, summarised as red, amber or green. Early versions of the canvas will be flagged as red – this shows that we are still eliciting and analysing information and therefore it cannot (yet) be relied upon. Later iterations will normally be green.
- **Problem/opportunity description:** A concise and precise statement of the problem or opportunity, as discussed in Section 2.2.
- **Benefits/measures of success:** The *outcomes* we are looking to achieve, often stated as CSFs and KPIs.

- **Concept-level requirements:** A very short summary of any key high level requirements that have been identified – these won't be extensive or exhaustive at this stage, but it is useful to capture any particularly important requirements that have been uncovered that will fundamentally shape the choice of solution.

- **Indicative scope:** An indication of the problem's scope, often shown using a business use case diagram.

- **Potential solution options identified:** A list of the short-listed solution options identified.

- **Appendices:** Attachments or links to other relevant documents.

- **CARID log:** An attached (or linked) constraints, assumptions, risks, issues and dependencies log.

- **Recommended next steps:** A summary of the recommended next steps that should be taken.

It is important to note that the problem canvas is a *summary of the problem, scope and solution.* It is not the *only* document that will be produced, and other documents can (and should) be added or linked to it as needed.

Bringing it all together: the one-page 'problem canvas'

Example: problem canvas

Problem name	**Demand Management**	Canvas ID	1203-18
Canvas author	Steven Thompson	Canvas version	1.0

Problem/Opportunity description

The problem of an increase in complaints due to an inability to process customer orders quickly enough during peak periods

Affects our customers (who are disappointed), our warehouse staff (who cannot keep up with demand) and our call centre staff (who have to deal with unhappy customers)

The impact of which is cancelled orders, reputational damage and increased complaints - all of which lead to increased operational costs and a reduction in profits

A successful solution would ensure that we can predict and manage demand, allowing us to dispatch orders in a timely fashion, leading to increased customer satisfaction, reduced operational costs and, ultimately, higher profits

Concept-level requirements

Summary:

The following high-level requirements have been noted as being of particular importance:

- Ability to deal with multiple currencies and foreign exchange (core currencies GBP, EUR, USD)
- Solution shall be available between core hours of 08:00–20:00 GMT – level of acceptable availability within these times TBC

Indicative scope

Potential solution options identified:

Option	Comment
Implement new order management system and process	Likely to be effective, but high initial investment
Offer incentive for 'no-rush' delivery (7-day delivery)	Would enable demand to be levelled or smoothed
Scale up: employ more staff	Discounted - would not solve root cause; however, may be useful as a short-term (temporary) fix
Do nothing	Discounted - would lead to decreasing profits

Source: Blackmetric Business Solutions

Portfolio	XYZ Portfolio	Sponsor	Kelly Carter	Confidence:
Date	1 January	Status	Submitted for review	**Green**

Benefits/Measures of success

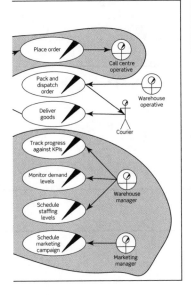

Attach further information/appendices here

Including confidence rationale, additional requirements, artefacts etc

Attach CARID log here

(constraints, assumptions, risks, issues, dependencies)

Recommended next steps

1. Due to the size of investment, carry out a full feasibility study to establish which potential solution is most appropriate

2. Elicit, analyse and document high level requirements

3. Create outline business case

Resources required

Estimated completion date: 1 March

How

1. Build the canvas up iteratively, as you go through the problem-solving process.

2. Bring it to meetings so that stakeholders become familiar with the format.

3. Use it to create a common view of the problem.

4. Add links and attachments as needed.

5. Feel free to embellish and adapt the template to meet your specific circumstances.

Reflection

- How did it work?

- What will I do next time?

6.2 Gaining consensus

Why

As we have alluded to throughout the book, problems can arise when different perceptions of a problem situation are not openly discussed, debated and reconciled. The problem canvas, on a single page, helps to trigger these conversations. It provides us with the opportunity to validate that we have a common view on the problem (and scope), and move forward with confidence that we have a genuine consensus.

Knowledge briefing

A problem canvas can normally be reviewed by convening a short meeting or workshop with the relevant interested parties. Unless stakeholders have worked with a problem canvas before, it is likely that the format will require some explanation, and it is worth allowing time for this at the beginning of the session. During the workshop itself, it is useful to walk the group through each section of the problem canvas, ensuring that opinions and perspectives are aligned.

Towards the end of the session, it is worth asking the sponsor to provide a formal sign-off during the workshop – this provides a formal 'line in the sand' and means that we can consider the document as approved.

If you have been building the canvas iteratively, during the problem-solving process, the review and validation should be relatively straightforward. Our stakeholders will have seen each *element* of the canvas previously, but this is our opportunity to showcase the whole document (and ensure that nothing has been missed or misunderstood).

Bringing it all together: the one-page 'problem canvas'

Source: iQoncept/Shutterstock

How

1. Refer back to the stakeholder analysis that you conducted earlier (see Section 1.4 and Section 4.2).

2. Consider who needs to be involved in validating the canvas.

3. Convene a workshop. Start by briefly explaining the purpose and format of the canvas.

4. Walk the stakeholders through each section of the canvas.

5. Have supplementary information/documents ready in case there are questions.

6. Discuss and aim to resolve any differences of opinion or conflict that arise.

7. Make any necessary amendments to the canvas.

8. Ask the sponsor to 'sign off' the document to indicate that they are happy with its accuracy.

9. Store the document in a central location that all relevant stakeholders can access.

Reflection

- How did it work?

[ ]

- What will I do next time?

[ ]

6.3 The canvas as an internal sales tool

Why

All but the most simple of problem-solving activities will require us to collaborate with others within (and sometimes outside of) our organisations. We may find ourselves in a situation where we need to *influence* somebody even though we have no direct *authority*.

The canvas can be a useful tool to help us gain influence and to 'sell' the problem-solving activities to those who we need to collaborate with.

Knowledge briefing

We often talk of 'stakeholders' in problem-solving initiatives. As we described in section 1.4, a stakeholder can be defined as:

'A group or individual with a relationship to the change, the need, or the solution.'

(International Institute of Business Analysis (IIBA), 2015)

This definition is broad, and it is quite possible that some individual stakeholders who will be *impacted* by the change may not have been directly *involved* in defining the problem canvas. Depending on the change, examples might include:

- Customers
- Suppliers
- Regulators
- Partners
- End-users and front-line staff
- Middle managers
- Neighbouring businesses
- Local authorities/governments

It is important that key stakeholder groups are brought up to speed, and also that we take the opportunity to elicit their opinions and views. It is important that we revisit our stakeholder engagement plan, and consider *which* stakeholders we particularly need to spend time with. As the problem-solving initiative continues, we will undoubtedly need to rely on their expertise to help us drill down and understand the nuances of the problem, so bringing them on board early is crucial.

Source: StockLite/Shutterstock

How

Revisit the stakeholder engagement plan

Firstly, it is crucial to revisit the stakeholder engagement plan and update it regularly, but it is particularly crucial to revisit it once the problem canvas is nearing completion. Good questions to ask are:

- 'Has the stakeholder landscape changed?'
- 'Does anyone else need to be involved?'
- 'Who is impacted or interested in this problem?'
- 'Who will be impacted or interested in the solutions we are proposing?'

It is important to remember that, although the problem canvas has now been completed, it *can* still be changed. If a new stakeholder appears on the radar, it is not too late to incorporate their views, or to incorporate crucial information that they may be able to provide! However, in reality, at this stage it is usual that the *big* decisions have been made robustly – and if we have carried out our problem analysis well, then any changes are likely to be minor.

Put together a communication plan

If you haven't already considered *how* you'll communicate with each stakeholder group, it is well worth spending time doing so now. Different stakeholders will benefit from different types of communication – building on the stakeholder map described in Section 1.4, we might utilise the following types of communication, shown in the table below.

Consider the message to convey

When communicating out details of a potential change, it is usual that some people may be initially resistant. It is worth spending time with our stakeholders to understand their concerns, and to

Bringing it all together: the one-page 'problem canvas'

Stakeholder influence	Impact of problem or solution on stakeholder	Type of communication	Example
High	High	Frequent, face to face where possible	Meetings, workshops, one-to-one conversations
High	Low	Regular consultation	Provide regular updates via e-mail Scheduled and ad-hoc meetings
Low	High	Regular information and opportunity to elicit thoughts/ commitment	Workshops Focus groups Roadshows Questionnaires
Low	Low	One-to-many 'broadcast'	E-mail newsletter Staff bulletins

do what we can to allay them. It is useful to take each stakeholder group and think WIIFM ('What's in it for me?'). If we can clearly articulate the benefits that solutions we are proposing will have for them, we are far more likely to bring them on board.

Communicate - often!

Finally, it has to be said that a communication plan is *no use* if it sits on the shelf collecting dust. Work with your colleagues to ensure that the communication happens, and ensure that any feedback that is received is considered and incorporated accordingly.

Reflection

- How did it work?

- What will I do next time?

References

International Institute of Business Analysis (IIBA), 2015. *A Guide to the Business Analysis Body of Knowledge® (BABOK® Guide)*, v3. Toronto: IIBA.

6.4 Gain commitment

Why

'Individual commitment to a group effort – that is what makes a team work, a company work, a society work, a civilisation work.'

(Vince Lombardi)

Solving any kind of problem is a group effort. Up until now, we have been focussed on thoroughly analysing the problem and imagining possible solutions. This is hard enough work – but actually *implementing* a solution can be quite difficult. This will often involve a coordinated effort from a wide range of people – this might include people who are involved in *implementing* the change as well as those *operating* the systems and processes that are affected by the change. For example, if part of our solution involves changing a process and making changes to an IT system, we would need action to be taken by developers, testers, process experts and so forth. Of equal importance, we'd need the end-users 'on the ground' to *use* the new systems and processes once they were rolled out. Therefore, gaining commitment from the relevant people is crucial.

Bringing it all together: the one-page 'problem canvas'

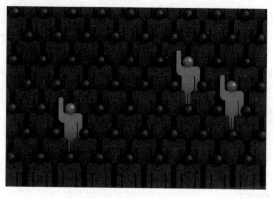

Source: cybrain/Shutterstock

Knowledge briefing

In the context of problem solving, we can consider at least three types of commitment that it would be useful for us to seek:

- **Getting it off the ground (commitment to the problem-solving initiative itself):** This type of commitment implies that the stakeholder approves and supports the need for change. They will provide resource to help assess the problem, and won't try to 'block' our activities.

- **Making it happen (commitment to action):** As well as a broad support for the initiative, we may need to gain commitment to individual *actions*.

- **Making it stick (commitment to longevity of the solution):** This type of commitment ensures that the solution (whatever it may be) is used and utilised on an ongoing basis. It ensures that teams don't creep back to old ways of working, whereby they inadvertently cause the problem to re-emerge.

How

Planning regular communication, as discussed in the previous section is absolutely key. This will help us to ensure that our stakeholders have a clear and unified view on what problem we are trying to solve. However, it is important that we also *ask for commitment*.

At the beginning of a problem-solving initiative we might ask a stakeholder to set aside a certain amount of time, so that we can be sure that they can actively participate in our analysis. Once a solution has been chosen, it is useful to put together a clear milestone plan, showing who is responsible for what, and explicitly asking people whether they feel able to commit to the necessary actions. A tool for framing this discussion is the RACI matrix. An example is illustrated below:

Task	Matt S	Becky C	Steve D	Bianca D	Carly T
Consult with customer services team	A	R	C	C	C
Measure number of missed sales to validate chosen solution	I	I		R/A	
Document new process	I	I	R/A		C
Test new process	A	I	I	R	C

Against each task, the RACI matrix shows who is:

R	Responsible	The person that is responsible for doing the task
A	Accountable	The person who is accountable for the task happening, and who will define the parameters and quality levels under which it should be undertaken (e.g. a senior manager or sponsor)
C	Consulted	An individual who should be consulted whilst the task is being undertaken
I	Informed	An individual who should be informed about the result of the task (often once it is completed)

This ensures that there is clear accountability and responsibility, and ensures that tasks do not 'fall between the gaps'. In particular, if there is no 'R' against a task, this means that *nobody* is responsible for it – so it won't actually take place! It can also ensure that we are able to have conversations with each stakeholder and ensure they are *willing* and *able* to undertake the tasks assigned to them. Gaining this commitment is extremely useful.

Beyond the RACI chart, it is also useful to ensure that the change 'sticks' – this requires ongoing expertise and input and is discussed further in Chapter 7.

Reflection

- How did it work?

- What will I do next time?

6.5 Plan the next steps

Why

A problem canvas provides a shared space for exploring and agreeing on potential solutions. However, for our problem-solving efforts to be successful we need to go ahead and *implement* the solution. It's crucial that we have a clear idea on the concrete next steps that are taken.

Knowledge briefing

A useful accompaniment to a problem canvas is a *milestone plan* or *schedule*. This should show the key activities and deliverables that are required to support the next steps. These are likely to complement and feed into the RACI matrix mentioned in the previous section.

A good schedule will show:

- Estimated effort/duration of each task
- The key activities
- The key milestones and deliverables
- The types of people and resources required
- The dependencies

How

Brainstorm the next tasks that are required, and write each one on a Post-it Note. Arrange these into the necessary order, and consider the dependencies between them. Some tasks are likely to require other tasks to have been completed first, and it's important that this is planned for. This brainstorming is often best carried out in a group – and usually several iterations will be required to refine the plan. It is likely that we'll start high-level, but delve into more detail over time.

Continuing with the example of a mail-order retailer mentioned earlier, we might recommend a solution which involves implementing enhanced web presence. We might conclude that the next steps would be:

1. Elicit and document our requirements for the enhanced website.

2. Engage three potential suppliers.

3. Get three quotes.

4. Compare and rank each supplier.

5. Make a decision over the best supplier.

6. Negotiate a contract.

7. Sign contract and approve work.

8. Supervise work.

9. Test website.

10. Sign off work as complete.

It is likely that as we discuss this plan with stakeholders, we'll uncover more details and more granular tasks – but this is a practical starting point. It is worth considering, at each stage, what the *deliverable* will be – i.e. what will the task *create* or *modify?* Specifying these deliverables can help make the plan crystal clear and ensure that expectations are aligned.

We may choose to create a Gantt chart (named after Henry Gantt, who developed the technique in the early 20th century). A Gantt chart clearly shows the tasks, expected duration, dependencies and milestones/deliverables – an example is included in the table below.

As you can see from the example above, as well as showing activities, the Gantt chart also shows the *type* and number of resources required, and can be used for tracking and communicating progress. The Gantt chart above is simplified, and shows time in *weeks* on the right hand side diagram – for more granular tasks it can be useful to show elapsed time in days.

It should be noted that if you are working alongside a dedicated project manager, they will be able to lead the planning of activities described above, and on larger initiatives will be able to bring useful additional project management methodologies and discipline to the endeavour.

ID	Task	Responsible	Effort	Duration	Start	End
T1	Elicit and document our requirements for the enhanced web	JS	10	18	01-Nov	28-Nov
T2	Engage 3 potential suppliers	JS	1	10	15-Nov	28-Nov
T3	Suppliers develop estimates/proposal	Suppliers	n/a	10	29-Nov	12-Dec
T4	Provide support during estimation/proposal lifecycle	JS	2	10	29-Nov	12-Dec
T5	Receive 3 quotes from suppliers	JS	0.5	0	13-Dec	13-Dec
T6	Compare and rank each supplier	JS, SD, BD	5	10	13-Dec	26-Dec
T7	*Holiday Period: Blocked Out*	All		11	22-Dec	02-Jan
T8	Make a decision over the best supplier	JS, SD, BD	1	0	03-Jan	03-Jan
T9	Negotiate a contract	IM	3	15	03-Jan	23-Jan
T10	Sign contract and approve work	SD	0.25	0	24-Jan	24-Jan
T11	*Lead time whilst supplier ramps up*	n/a	n/a	10	24-Jan	06-Feb
T12	Supervise work	JS, BD	9.75	39	07-Feb	02-Apr
T13	Test website	JS, BD	15	10	03-Apr	16-Apr
T14	Bug fixing and release	Supplier	n/a	10	17-Apr	30-Apr
T15	Sign off work as complete	JS	05	0	01-May	01-May

Week commencing: 01-Nov, 08-Nov, 15-Nov, 22-Nov, 29-Nov, 06-Dec, 13-Dec, 20-Dec, 27-Dec, 03-Jan, 10-Jan, 17-Jan, 24-Jan, 31-Jan, 07-Feb, 14-Feb, 21-Feb, 28-Feb, 06-Mar, 13-Mar, 20-Mar, 27-Mar, 03-Apr, 10-Apr, 17-Apr, 24-Apr, 01-May, 08-May

Reflection

- How did it work?

- What will I do next time?

6.6 Beware risks

Why

However we decide to solve a problem, it is likely that there will be some inherent *risks*. If these risks materialise, they could not only scupper our problem-solving initiative, they may have a negative impact on our team or even our whole business. Before we jump head-first into implementing a solution, it is important that we take time to appreciate and understand these risks, and consider what actions we might take to cater for them.

Source: Gunnar Pippel/Shutterstock

Knowledge briefing

A risk can be defined as:

> *'The effect of uncertainty on the value of a change, a solution, or the enterprise.'*
>
> (International Institute of Business Analysis (IIBA), 2015)

When capturing potential risks, it is useful to consider the *risk event* as well as its *consequence*. For example, a risk event might be that 'Customers do not take up our new online ordering system at the rate that we have projected'. The consequence may be 'We don't save as much in administrative costs as we have hoped'.

It is also worth thinking about the *probability* that the risk will occur and the *impact* that would be caused if it would occur. Clearly, more time will be spent worrying about risks that are highly probable, and less will be spent on improbable/low impact risks.

For each risk, we should consider a *risk modification strategy*. The type of modification strategies we can consider include:

- **Avoid:** Change course so the risk no longer applies.
- **Mitigate:** Take steps to lessen the impact if the risk does occur.
- **Transfer:** Transfer, insure or outsource the risk to another party.
- **Accept:** Take no specific action (often relevant for very low probability and low impact risks).

As an illustration of the different risk modification strategies, let's imagine we were about to travel by car, but we were worried about the risk of a car accident occurring. We could *avoid* the risk by deciding against getting in the car, and taking the train instead – but by doing so, we introduce a different set of risks. We could *mitigate* the risk by ensuring that the car has seatbelts, airbags and other safety features. This won't stop an accident occurring, but it will lessen the impact if it does. We're also likely to *transfer* some of the risk by *insuring* the car – so any damage caused to other property is covered by an insurance company. We could of course choose to simply *accept* the risk and get in the car without any of those risk modification strategies being in place.

How

Work with stakeholders to create a list of potential risks. Capture these so that they can be actively managed. Consider the probability, impact and the risk modification strategy for each. A possible template is shown in the table below.

The template includes the following sections:

1. **ID:** An identifier for the risk that allows it to be uniquely identified.
2. **Risk event:** A description of the risk event itself.
3. **Consequence:** What happens if the risk occurs?
4. **Probability:** The likelihood that the risk will occur (perhaps on a scale of 1–10).
5. **Impact:** The level of impact that would be caused if the risk occurred (perhaps on a scale of 1–10).
6. **Risk score:** An overall score for the risk – often derived by multiplying risk score and impact, although it is possible to use more complicated scoring mechanisms also.
7. **Risk modification:** Whether to avoid, mitigate, transfer or accept the risk – and the specific action necessary to do so.
8. **Owner:** The person accountable for the risk and ensuring any modifying action is taken.
9. **Residual risk:** What level of risk remains if the risk modification action is taken?

ID#	Risk event	Consequence	Probability	Impact	Risk score	Risk modification	Owner	Residual risk
R01	Our largest customer cannot integrate with the proposed online system	We lose orders, so revenue (and profit) drops	Low 2	High 8	Medium 16	Avoid: Work closely with top customer to ensure integration will work	John Smith	Low

Example of risk register. Format derived from International Institute of Business Analysis (IIBA), 2015. *A Guide to the Business Analysis Body of Knowledge® (BABOK® Guide)*, v3. Toronto: IIBA

The risk register ensures that everyone has a common view of the potential risks and pitfalls. It should be regularly revisited, with new risks being added as soon as they are identified. Somebody – perhaps a project manager – should be tasked with keeping it up to date and also ensuring that the relevant risk modification actions are taken. This useful action will help minimise the chances of risks scuppering our progress!

Reflection

• How did it work?

• What will I do next time?

References

International Institute of Business Analysis (IIBA), 2015. *A Guide to the Business Analysis Body of Knowledge® (BABOK® Guide)*, v3. Toronto: IIBA.

6.7 A problem canvas is a great place to start (but the hard work is yet to come)

Why

Creating a problem canvas provides a way for us to concisely and precisely define and discuss a problem. However, it is important for us and our stakeholders to realise that it is only the *start* of the problem-solving process. It would be very easy to get caught in a loop of 'analysis paralysis' – constantly refining and polishing the canvas – but in doing so we'd stray from our real objective of actually *solving* the problem!

It is therefore important that we recognise when the problem canvas is 'good enough', and start pushing towards the specific actions and next steps that are required (and that we discussed defining in Section 6.5).

Source: Michael D. Brown/Shutterstock

Knowledge briefing

The level of effort and analysis that will underpin a problem canvas will depend on the size of the problem and the risks associated with it. Clearly, a fairly simple and non-controversial problem may require just a few simple conversations and a roughly drawn problem statement to harbour agreement. Equally if the expected effort to fix the problem is very low, it would be disproportionate to spend excessive time thinking about the problem. However, when problems are particularly large, complex, chaotic or risky, more effort will need to be spent on understanding and analysing the situation.

How

When considering how much effort and time to spend on the analysis that feeds into the problem canvas (and when considering how much 'polishing' to do) consider:

1. How much effort is involved in implementing a solution? If it's low effort and low risk, then don't spend excessive time polishing the canvas.

2. What are the risks associated with the solution(s)? If there are numerous, or if there are critical/high-impact risks, more up-front risk analysis may be sensible.

3. Consider the culture of the organisation. What level of governance does it require? Some organisations require fully completed and documented analysis before action – in others a more lightweight approach may be appropriate.

4. Consider the urgency of the problem. Is there benefit in doing *something* quickly, measuring the results, learning and tweaking? Or is it better to wait until there is more certainty.

5. What are the opportunity costs? If we take the problem-solving action, what else *can't* we do? What do we give up?

6. Are the stakeholders and key contributors bought into the actions that are required?

7. Is everyone willing and able to take the next steps?

These questions will help you to assess whether the problem canvas is *ready*. If it is, it is important that we move forward and execute the necessary actions to actually *solve* the problem. This is often a joint effort, and if there are many people involved, ensuring that somebody is acting as 'project manager' can be extremely useful. The project manager will ensure that the right people are undertaking the right activities at the right time, and will keep the problem-solving initiative on track.

Reflection

- How did it work?

- What will I do next time?

Chapter 7

Making sure problems stay solved: implementing, measuring success and pivoting

7. Making sure problems stay solved: implementing, measuring success and pivoting

7.1 What happens after the problem canvas is written?

Even if you work in the smallest and most stable of organisations, it is likely that there will be *several* problem-solving initiatives being undertaken simultaneously. When resources are scarce, it will be necessary to determine *which* problems to address first, and which solutions should be implemented with most urgency.

With multiple problems being considered, we can create multiple problem canvases. This allows us to *prioritise* each problem, and allows a decision to be made over which problem(s) to address first. This also enables us to consider the dependencies between problem-solving initiatives, for example, some problems may need to be solved before others can be addressed.

Source: rnl/Shutterstock

Do this

Encourage others who are working on problem-solving initiatives to create a problem canvas for their projects. Create an environment where problem canvases can be compared and prioritised against each other – the remainder of the chapter will provide tips and tricks to achieve this.

7.2 Compare and prioritise problems

As outlined in the previous section, it is likely that there will be many problems vying for our attention. Rather than trying to solve *every* problem, and spreading ourselves too thinly, it is important to compare which problems we will focus on. It can be extremely valuable to put conscious thought into how you will ensure that each canvas is correctly prioritised and aligned with your organisation's overall strategic direction.

Source: pedrosala/Shutterstock

Do this

Create a forum for reviewing/discussing problem canvasses. Create a set of decision criteria which will help the team decide which problems warrant attention.

7.3 Inspire action: keeping up the momentum to implement a solution

Very small problem-solving initiatives may require just a few hours effort to define and resolve. Large scale initiatives may take significant amounts of time, investment and resources. Two roles that are crucial for the success of problem-solving initiatives are the *business analyst* and the *project manager*. Much of what has been discussed in this book so far falls within the wider discipline of business analysis – and if you have been following it you have perhaps been unknowingly carrying out a range of business analysis tasks! It is important to acknowledge that this will be an ongoing role, and there will be more analysis work to follow. Alongside the business analysis work, on larger problem-solving initiatives it is useful to assign a project manager. These two roles will work hand-in hand to ensure that the *right thing* is done in the *right way*.

Source: mypokcik/Shutterstock

Do this

Ensure that it is clear who will undertake the ongoing business analysis responsibility for the problem-solving initiative, and who will undertake the ongoing project management work. Ensure there is continuity wherever possible. Work with the project manager to build on the plan that has been created previously, and consider holding a 'kick off' event to inspire action in those who need to be involved with the implementation of the chosen solution.

7.4 Get ready to measure success

Problem-solving initiatives are carried out to create some sort of benefit. Once we have implemented a solution, it is important that we measure what benefits have accrued. If the anticipated benefits haven't been realised, we might find that further refinement (or incremental tweaking) will lead to further benefits being released.

Being able to assess the benefits is predicated on us having measured a baseline *before* the change was implemented. Additionally, we may need to build in systems or processes for regularly capturing the data needed to carry out the ongoing measurements. This should be built into our solution ideally from the moment it is implemented.

Source: Andrey_Kuzmin/Shutterstock

Do this

Build on the KPIs to ensure that specific metrics and targets are set. Measure a baseline, and once the change is implemented, ensure that regular measurements are taken to track progress.

7.5 Stay close to ensure problems don't recur

Planning and implementing change takes a significant amount of effort – but making change stick can be even trickier. It would be something of an 'own goal' if we spent time and money implementing a solution, only for key stakeholders to abandon use of the solution within weeks (or months).

To avoid this happening, it is crucial that we embed the change – we make it part of 'the way we do things here'. This involves clear and regular communication with affected stakeholder groups, and also regular support and monitoring *after* the change has been implemented. It is important that we don't implement change and walk away.

Source: Syda Productions/Shutterstock

Do this

Ensure there is a clear communication and engagement plan, and that relevant support is provided after the change is implemented. Monitor regularly to look for opportunities for further improvement and to ensure that the solution is sufficiently embedded.

7.6 Seek further opportunities to tweak and pivot

Problem solving doesn't have to be a one-off activity, and once we have implemented a solution there will often be ample opportunities for incremental tweaks. We may hypothesise that a certain solution will be effective, but until we have *tried* it we won't know for sure. It is therefore crucial that we regularly measure and check the benefits that have accrued, and tweak or change the solution when necessary. In order to do this it is very useful to regularly visit the affected business area and see the solution in action with our own eyes – we can work with (and encourage) those involved day-to-day to come up with incremental changes, and empower them to implement them.

Source: push-to-grave/Shutterstock

Do this

Ensure that regular measurements are taken to ensure that the solution is operating effectively and that the anticipated benefits are accruing. Actively look for ways to improve further, and encourage others to do the same.

7.7 Embed the practice of continuous improvement

As alluded to in the previous section, problem solving is often an ongoing process, and it is useful to embed not just a *change* but also to encourage continuous improvement to take place – across all relevant processes. This can start small, perhaps with a suggestion scheme. For very small problems, the canvas may provide a useful set of questions to ask – although if a document is produced it may be very lightweight indeed. For small scale problems, we may encourage people to carry out controlled experiments and see how incremental interventions work.

All of this relies on us and our stakeholders feeling empowered to raise suggestions and to highlight problems. Problem-solving initiatives are a useful way of starting to embed this ethos into a business area.

Source: Gines Valera Marin/Shutterstock

Do this

When working on a problem-solving initiative, consider whether the teams involved currently assess their work practices to look for regular improvements. If not, consider whether this could be an opportunity to encourage the adoption of these processes.

7.1 What happens after the problem canvas is written?

Why

As outlined in the previous chapter, writing a problem canvas is an extremely valuable starting point, but there is often significant work to follow. In particular, it is likely that there will be *multiple* problems and opportunities being examined at any one time and thought must be put into prioritising the most important. Also, as soon as any kind of solution is implemented, it will be useful to monitor the success so that we can ensure we are maximising the benefit. This entire chapter is dedicated to ensuring we select the right problems to address and ensuring that they stay solved!

Knowledge briefing

In every organisation resources are finite and it isn't possible to adopt every good idea or solve every problem. Some problems and potential solutions might not be considered 'big' enough to spend precious time and resources investigating further, and some potential solutions might be out of line with the organisation's overall strategy. Creating a problem canvas for each problem allows early problem prioritisation to take place. This ensures that effort is focussed on solving those problems and solutions that will yield most benefit. It can be useful to imagine four distinct sets of activities:

Making sure problems stay solved

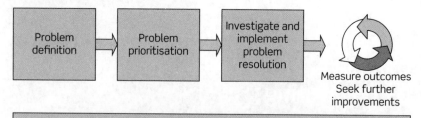

Ongoing analysis and refinement

- **Problem (and outcome) definition:** This involves defining the problem and the desired outcomes. A problem canvas is an extremely valuable starting point that can be iteratively built upon.

- **Problem prioritisation:** Prioritisation involves establishing *which* problem or problems should be addressed, and which are the most urgent. This is likely to be based on a range of criteria including cost, benefit, risks and so on.

- **Investigate and implement problem resolution:** Once commitment has been made to address a particular problem, the physical implementation of the solution will begin. This may involve further detailed investigation and specification of a solution, and is likely to require additional business analysis expertise.

- **Measure outcomes and seek further improvements:** After a solution has been implemented, it is critical that we *measure* success. There may be other incremental opportunities for improvement that can be taken.

The level of formality and the time spent on each task will vary depending on the organisational context, the urgency and the nature (and urgency) of the problem. More formal project and system development lifecycles can be used where more formality is required – useful resources can be found in the 'References and further reading' section.

How

1. Ensure that problems are compared, contrasted and prioritised (see Section 7.2).

2. Engage and inspire those that need to take action (see Section 7.3).

3. Collect data and measure success (see Section 7.4).

4. Monitor performance data to ensure problems don't recur (see Section 7.5).

5. Look for opportunities to tweak things further (see Section 7.6).

6. Empower people to make small incremental changes, whilst keeping the bigger picture in mind (see Section 7.7).

Reflection

- How did it work?

- What will I do next time?

7.2 Compare and prioritise problems

Why

There are often a whole range of problems and opportunities in an organisation's ecosystem, each vying for our attention.

Organisations are likely to have limited resources, and although every problem statement will look important when viewed in isolation, it is important to pick the key initiatives that are most important or that will be most beneficial to the organisation.

It is also crucial to take a step back and look at our problem-solving initiatives holistically. It's crucial that we make sure the *solutions* that we are implementing are consistent and compatible with the organisation's overall strategy. It's also useful to consider the knock-on impacts of any actions that we might take in our problem-solving initiative.

Source: Nelson Marques/Shutterstock

Knowledge briefing

Every solution we implement and every change we make will form part of a bigger business system. When considering which problems to address and which solutions to implement, it's important that we think holistically and consider the bigger picture. The four-view model discussed in Section 1.2 can be useful, as it encourages us to think about people, process, organisation *and* IT.

When problem solving, we should be careful not to transfer the problem elsewhere (to another unsuspecting team or department!). Drawing on the mail-order retailer example we have referred to several times in the book, there would be no point solving *one* problem ('too many out of stock items') by renting a bigger warehouse, if that meant causing another problem ('unsustainable fixed costs'). It is therefore imperative that we *prioritise* our portfolio of problem canvasses, looking for strategic alignment, costs, benefits and knock-on impacts.

How

1. **Create a forum for reviewing/discussing problem canvasses:** Create a space where problem canvasses can be discussed and reviewed. This could be a regular (but short) meeting, or an online discussion forum where opinions of the relevant stakeholders can be sought. Key decision-makers and experts from different areas of the organisation should be invited – they will bring useful perspectives to the fore.

2. **Decide how to decide:** Create a set of decision criteria that will help the forum decide which problems to address, and which to defer or park. Criteria may include considering costs, benefits, risks and other relevant factors.

3. **Ensure strategic alignment:** Before taking a problem canvas to the forum, the 'problem owner' should ensure that the solution that is being recommended aligns with the organisation's stated strategy. This includes ensuring alignment with broad market strategies, as well as any internal architectural or technical strategies. It would be inconsistent, for example, to suggest launching a 'low-cost, low-service' proposition if an organisation's strategy specifically targets the prestige market. Of course, if the solution *is* really compelling, then this might be a prompt to *revisit* the organisation's strategy – but this should be considered separately.

4. **Prioritise:** Problem canvasses should be prioritised, with the most valuable/urgent being given preference. When prioritising, it is worth considering what is most important for *your* organisation. There are many dimensions that might be considered including:
   - Tangible business benefit: Which option will generate the greatest (or quickest) return, measured in financial or other measurable terms. Example: 'Increase sales by 5 per cent, leading to additional revenue of £100,000 in year 1'.

- Intangible business benefit: What non-quantifiable (or non-predictable) returns are associated with each option. Example: 'Better brand awareness amongst our customer base'.

- Risk: How much risk is associated with each option, and how much risk are we willing to take?

- Customer benefit: Which of the options would be best perceived by our customers?

- Urgency: Which is most urgent or time critical? Example: Getting a crucial issue resolved in a retail company before Christmas.

- Business environment: Which option best fits with the external business environment, as explored in the STEEPLE analysis. There may be some changes that are imposed – e.g. regulatory changes – that *have* to be adopted.

5. **Consistency:** Finally, it is worth ensuring that there is consistency between the canvasses that are selected. It is important that problem-solving initiatives complement each other and do not conflict or contradict each other.

Often the prioritisation effort will involve discussion, debate, further analysis and compromise. Ensuring that the relevant voices are heard in this process is important, and will ensure that the organisation pursues the problem-solving options that give them best bang for their buck.

Reflection

- How did it work?

- What will I do next time?

7.3 Inspire action: keeping up the momentum to implement a solution

Why

Problem-solving initiatives come in all shapes and sizes. Smaller problems may be solvable with just a few hours' effort – but the larger, more thorny problems that we face in today's business may require solutions that take weeks or months to implement. In some cases we might need to implement experimental solutions, and *see* if they work, then adapt them and tweak them based on our learning.

All of this takes focussed effort over a period of time. In Section 6.4 we talked about gaining commitment for those who need to take action. An ongoing challenge is to ensure that everyone involved stays on track, and stays focussed on the end-goal. Particularly with problem-solving initiatives, this can be problematic. It can be useful to engage some specialist roles to help us.

Source: volk6/Shutterstock

Knowledge briefing

On larger problem-solving initiatives, two roles that you will want to ensure stay filled are those of the business analyst and project manager. The tasks, tools and techniques mentioned in this book largely fall within the wider discipline of business analysis – so if you have followed the steps suggested in this book, you have (perhaps unknowingly) carried out elements of a business analysis role!

The discipline of business analysis is defined by the International Institute of Business Analysis as:

> 'The practice of enabling change in the context of an enterprise by defining needs and recommending solutions that deliver value to stakeholders.'
>
> (International Institute of Business Analysis (IIBA), 2015)

In *Business Analysis* (3rd edition), Paul et al describe the role as:

> 'An advisory role which has the responsibility for investigating and analysing business situations, identifying and evaluating options for improving business systems, elaborating and defining requirements, and ensuring the effective implementation and use of information systems in line with the needs of the business.'
>
> (Paul, Cadle and Yeates, 2014)

It is normal practice for large organisations to have specialist business analysts on-hand to help – and in many organisations there are people fulfilling similar or identical roles (even though they may not have the job title). The important thing is to make sure *someone* is fulfilling the role, and that this person has the relevant skills and is given the relevant autonomy and scope.

Another crucial role is that of the project manager. Project management is defined by the Association for Project Management as:

'Project management is the application of processes, methods, knowledge, skills and experience to achieve the project objectives.'

(Association for Project Management (APM), n.d.)

Dr Martin Barnes (APM President 2003–2012) observed that:

'At its most fundamental, project management is about people getting things done.'

(APM, n.d.)

The project manager and business analyst will work closely together to ensure success of the initiative, and will provide regular updates.

How

1. **Ensure there continues to be a lead business analyst:** Much of the problem analysis discussed in this book falls within the wider discipline of *business analysis* that is described above. As the problem-solving initiative goes forward, it is crucial to continue to have somebody on board who can analyse the detail of the situation and ensure that the solution is shaped to meet your needs. The role of business analysis starts long before the problem-solving initiative is formed, and continues long after the problem is defined. Ensure that consistent and sufficient analysis support is provided.

2. **Assign a project manager:** It is useful to have somebody who is responsible for managing the implementation of the solution. They will work alongside the business analyst to ensure successful delivery. The business analyst will ensure that the *right thing* is done – and the project manager will ensure that it's *done in the right way*. Two subtly different, but entirely complementary roles.

3. **Build on the plan:** A good project manager will work with the team to put together a project schedule, showing the tasks required and dependencies. This will build upon and enhance the Gantt chart and RACI matrix we discussed in Sections 6.4 and 6.5.

4. **Hold a 'kick-off' event:** Getting the relevant people together to critique and agree the updated and more detailed plan will help build additional commitment. It will also be the perfect opportunity to revisit and discuss potential risks or assumptions. Use the kick-off event to showcase the problem canvas, and ensure people have a laser-like focus on the goal that is being achieved. The business analyst is a perfect candidate to facilitate this session.

5. **Work the plan:** As the implementation effort continues, ensure that the project manager is keeping a tab on the activities that have been undertaken, the progress that has been made, and the deliverables that have been created. However, as Alfred Korzybski is reported to have commented: 'The map is not the territory'.

   Much in the same way that we wouldn't blindly follow a map if the terrain in front of us had flooded unexpectedly, we shouldn't follow a plan if we uncover unexpected problems or issues. The plan should *adapt* to the territory, and we should maintain constant vigilance against any unexpected surprises.

6. **Get regular feedback:** Ensure that a regular 'temperature check' is taken from people involved with the change. Do they *feel* they are making adequate progress? Are there any blockages? Are they still 'on board' and are they still willing and able to help? If they are very busy in their 'day job' this may affect their ability to help us with our initiative, and this is something we should be mindful of throughout.

7. **Communicate progress:** Ensure that regular communication takes place, so that people are aware of the challenges and successes. Ensure this information is shared in an appropriate way for the audience – in some situations a brief 'stand-up' meeting may be appropriate, in others a more formal meeting. Some stakeholders may simply need a regular e-mail (followed up by an occasional phone-call to check that everything is clear). Ensure the communication is tailored to the needs of the audience.

Reflection

- How did it work?

- What will I do next time?

References

Association for Project Management (APM), n.d. *What is Project Management?* Available at: https://www.apm.org.uk/WhatIsPM

International Institute of Business Analysis (IIBA), 2015. *A Guide to the Business Analysis Body of Knowledge® (BABOK® Guide), v3.* Toronto: IIBA.

Paul, D., Cadle, J. and Yeates, D. (eds), 2014. *Business Analysis.* Third Edition. Swindon: BCS.

7.4 Get ready to measure success

Why

The whole point of problem solving is to create some sort of benefit. Therefore, once a solution has been implemented, assuming we have solved the problem well, benefits should start to accrue. Prior to implementing the solution we will have forecast the likely benefits in the problem canvas, and for larger scale initiatives we may have carried out further analysis and created a formal business case document.

This is a crucial step but it is true to say that it will only be an *approximation* of the likely benefits. It is important that we measure our *actual* level of success.

Knowledge briefing

Measuring the success of a problem-solving initiative ensures that:

- The objectives have been met and the desired outcomes were achieved.
- The anticipated benefits have been realised.

In some cases, we may find that the anticipated benefits have not been realised, or the desired outcomes haven't been met. This can be for a number of reasons – perhaps the business environment changed around us. A competitor may have launched a new product or might have shifted strategy and started to target our customers. Or perhaps there were additional internal complexities – we ended up opening a 'can of worms' and although we were able to realise *some* benefit, perhaps the costs were higher than we expected.

Understanding the benefits that have (or haven't) been realised, and the costs that were incurred, helps us to estimate more accurately next time. It can also help us identify opportunities for tweaking or pivoting that may help us to realise *further* benefits.

How

The diagram below indicates an approach for ensuring that we can measure success.

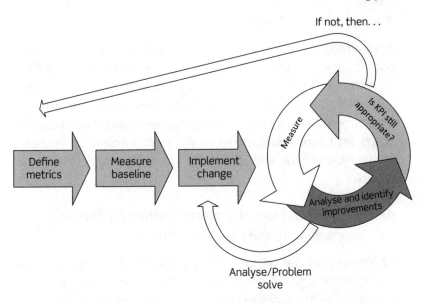

1. **Define metrics (and ensure mechanisms in place to measure them)**

The key to ensuring that benefits can be accurately measured is to clearly define *how* the measurement should be taken. For example, if a problem-solving initiative is intended to speed up an order dispatch process, it would be important to ensure there was a clear view on where the dispatch process starts and ends. Do we start timing the process from when the customer places their order to when the customer receives their order? Or from when the warehouse receive the order to when the item is loaded onto a van? Either measure will have pros and cons associated with it, but it is important to settle on one.

2. **Measure a baseline**

It is also crucial to ensure that there is an accurate baseline of data *before* the change is made. Drawing on the example mentioned above, it will be important to have average measurements of the time taken to dispatch an item *before* any solution is implemented. If this baseline data does not exist, it will be impossible to know for certain whether an improvement has been attained!

3. *Implement the change*

When crafting and implementing our solution thought should be put into ensuring that the relevant performance data is regularly collected. If the dispatch time is automatically collected, it can be queried and reported on regularly. This makes our benefits assessment much easier. This may involve adding data collection steps into processes, or ensuring that automated systems measure, capture and store the relevant metrics for later retrieval.

4. *Measure and identify opportunities for further improvement and consider KPIs*

Depending on the nature of the expected benefits, we may set up some type of 'dashboard' so that we can track progress regularly – with the ability to 'drill into' the data if we need further information. An example is shown in the table below.

In this example, any over- or under-performance can be highlighted for further consideration – the average dispatch time stands out as not being on track, so may warrant further investigation. Further changes or tweaks may be necessary to get back on track. Equally, lessons may be learned where *over-performance* has occurred.

Highlighting our progress in this way enables us to search for areas where further opportunities for improvement may exist. It is also useful to regularly consider and validate that the KPIs being gathered and the targets set are still appropriate. If the organisation's environment or strategy has changed, then it may be necessary to revisit the way that things are measured. This will involve re-baselining, and may involve implementing new data collection into the existing systems and processes.

KPI	Prior baseline (average)	January (forecast)	January (actual)	Variance	February (forecast)	February (actual)	Variance
Average speed of answer (phone calls)	1.5 mins	1 min	47 sec	–13 sec	45 sec	30 sec	–15 sec
Average dispatch time	75 hours	24 hours	25 hours	+1 hour	22 hours	22 hours	–
Sales volume (revenue)/ month	£123k	£150k	£155k	+ £5k	£160k	£161k	+£1k

Reflection

- How did it work?

```
┌─────────────────────────────────────────────────────┐
│                                                       │
│                                                       │
│                                                       │
│                                                       │
│                                                       │
│                                                       │
└─────────────────────────────────────────────────────┘
```

- What will I do next time?

```
┌─────────────────────────────────────────────────────┐
│                                                       │
│                                                       │
│                                                       │
│                                                       │
│                                                       │
│                                                       │
└─────────────────────────────────────────────────────┘
```

7.5 Stay close to ensure problems don't recur

Why

Having successfully 'solved' a problem, it is tempting to walk away and think that our work is complete. Yet if we let our attention wane, there is a danger that the problem will start to re-manifest itself and reoccur. It is crucial that we continue to monitor the situation and look out for warning signs.

Knowledge briefing

In *Leading Change* John Kotter describes *declaring victory too soon* as one significant reason why changes fail within organisations. He describes how change takes a time to 'sink in' within organisations. He points out that:

Source: Lord and Leverett/Pearson Education Ltd.

'Until changes sink down deeply into the culture . . . new approaches are fragile and subject to regression.'

(Kotter, 1996)

We have probably all seen situations like this occur in our own organisations. Ideas get raised, solutions get implemented, but they don't *stick*. Over time, people slowly revert to doing things the 'old way' and any potential benefits are lost.

There are a number of reasons why this may happen. Sometimes it may be that the solution wasn't well specified or perhaps the problem wasn't fully understood. Other times there may be a passive resistance to the change. Other times it can be that the change wasn't *reinforced* – there was no support *after* implementation and so the change fizzled out.

It is therefore crucial that we consider not only how to *communicate* the change but how to *support and sustain* the change.

How

1. **Refer to (and action) your communication and engagement plan:** The idea of communication planning was discussed in Section 6.3. The act of *creating* a communication plan is useful – but its utility is seriously diminished if it sits gathering dust in a drawer somewhere! Ensure that the team are actively revisiting, updating and *actioning* the communication plan throughout the problem-solving initiative. Communication efforts are likely to become of increased significance as you get closer to implementing a change.

2. **Keep communicating *after* implementation:** After a change has been implemented, it is still crucial to keep the lines of communication open. It is important to hear the views of those whose work has changed, and to take into account any further changes or tweaks that may be necessary. Keeping the lines of communication open also ensures that we can *reinforce* the change. We can remind people of any important nuances and subtleties.

3. **Monitor regularly:** As discussed in the previous section it is crucial to track progress. Regular monitoring and communication of these metrics will also help determine if the change has 'stuck'. If the metrics or KPIs start to 'wander back' to the previous benchmark, this *could* be a sign that people are reverting to old methods. This is an opportunity to investigate, discuss and understand why. By spotting this early, we have the opportunity to bring people on board.

Reflection

- How did it work?

- What will I do next time?

References

Kotter, J., 1996. *Leading Change*. Boston: Harvard Business Press.

7.6 Seek further opportunities to tweak and pivot

Why

Problem solving isn't normally a 'one-off' activity. When we implement a solution, we solve the problem that existed at a particular point in time. However, over time things change – our business environment changes around us, new technology becomes available, external regulations change and so on. We might find that a solution that once worked perfectly now needs to be tweaked. Or alternatively, during our monitoring activities, we might spot possibilities to make things work even better (which will allow us to realise further benefits).

It also has to be said that until a solution is put into service, we never really know *how* it will work. We may theorise, for example, that a brand new website will make the purchase process easier, and people will purchase more often. We might 'test' this idea before implementing it, and work with customer focus groups to understand their ideas and needs. Yet until we *launch* the website we can't be certain whether it will really have the desired effect, nor can we be sure of the *volume* of additional sales that it will generate. Therefore, building in the ability for further monitoring, tweaking and pivoting is crucial.

Knowledge briefing

The idea of 'pivoting' was popularised by authors such as Eric Ries. In *The Lean Startup*, Ries describes a pivot as:

> '[a] . . . structured course correction designed to test a new fundamental hypothesis about the product, strategy, and engine of growth.'

(Ries, 2011)

In this context, Ries is referring to higher level strategising, decision making and problem solving – perhaps whether to launch a new product in a new market, and if so what that product should look like. However, the fact remains that even on small yet important problem-solving initiatives we are *hypothesising* that our preferred solution will be effective. We carry out analysis to validate this in advance, but there will still be an element of risk – an element of the unknown. We could consider our chosen solution to be a *hypothesis of benefit* – we believe that it will be beneficial, and we have projected the potential figures, but until it is delivered we are unable to test it for sure.

Pivoting allows us to make large or small corrections, enabling us to stay on course. It involves focussing on the core *benefits* that we want to achieve.

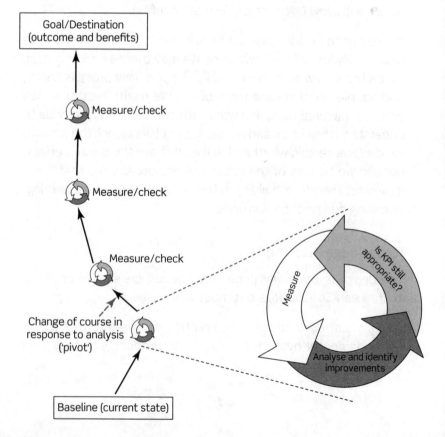

How

1. **Look at the data:** As we have described in Section 7.5, it is important to regularly monitor the performance of the chosen solution once it is in place. Make time to look at the data and spot any anomalies. This involves investigating both under-performance and over-performance. If performance increases, even temporarily, it can be useful to know why. Perhaps there is an opportunity to make this the new normal! If the performance is consistently better than we need, perhaps too much resource has been allocated, which can be better utilised elsewhere. It's also important to reflect on whether the KPI and target is still relevant and appropriate – if not, this may need revisiting too. The three-stage approach of *measuring, identifying improvements* and *checking whether the relevant KPIs are still appropriate* can be helpful here.

2. **Go and see with your own eyes:** Speak to people who are involved with the solution – what opportunities for improvement do they see? Work with them, perhaps for a day or more, to understand the environment and any constraints that they work under. This is an excellent way of building rapport, and also understanding whether there might be *other* problem areas that haven't (yet) been mentioned. It is also a very useful opportunity to see if the solution is *actually* working – sometimes we may find that there are 'exceptions' and 'workarounds' that haven't been mentioned or considered. By taking time to consider these we may well increase the overall efficiency and effectiveness of the solution.

3. **Pivot (propose a change):** Where there are opportunities for improvements, put forward the case for change. If the change is fairly small, this might be a simple quick conversation. If the change is larger in scale, it may be beneficial to put together an amended problem canvas. It is useful to set this expectation that there may be iterative changes/pivot-points early. With every pivot we get closer to solving the *whole* problem and maximising the organisational benefit!

Reflection

- How did it work?

```
┌─────────────────────────────────────────────────┐
│                                                   │
│                                                   │
│                                                   │
│                                                   │
│                                                   │
│                                                   │
└─────────────────────────────────────────────────┘
```

- What will I do next time?

```
┌─────────────────────────────────────────────────┐
│                                                   │
│                                                   │
│                                                   │
│                                                   │
│                                                   │
│                                                   │
└─────────────────────────────────────────────────┘
```

References

Ries, E., 2011. *The Lean Startup.* London: Portfolio Penguin.

7.7 Embed the practice of continuous improvement

Why

Problem solving is an ongoing activity, and problems exist at different levels. Some might be extremely large and wide ranging ('Our revenue has dropped by 25 per cent overnight – how do we address this?'), some might be much smaller and more localised ('This printer is continually jamming and it's taking up our time').

The problem-solving process described in this book can be adapted to work at just about any level. For large organisational changes, it can fit into a pre-project problem analysis phase (prior to a formal business case). For small 'tweaks' the template may provide a useful set of questions to ask – even if the document itself is kept very, very brief.

However, the intention is *not* for this to become a barrier to getting things done. Problem solving shouldn't be bureaucratic, and the problem-solving process (and the problem canvas) should *enable* high-quality decisions to be made over which solutions to choose. It should maximise benefits without slowing things down. Indeed, it may even *speed things up* – once a firm decision has been made on a solution, the problem-solving initiative can accelerate.

All of this is predicated on the fact that people are *looking* for problems to solve. So often in organisations, people 'get used to' particular ways of working. It is easy to become blind to the inefficiencies of a system or process if you have been working the same way for 20 years. Indeed, it can be difficult to imagine *any other* way of working.

For problem solving to be of maximum effect, it's useful to empower the team and create an ongoing focus on continuous improvement.

Source: Gines Valera Marin/Shutterstock

Knowledge briefing

Continuous improvement can be defined as:

> ' . . . *an ongoing effort to improve products, services or processes. These efforts can seek "incremental"*

237

> *improvement over time or "breakthrough" improvement all at once.'*

(American Society for Quality, n.d.)

Many continuous improvement philosophies and methodologies exist including Lean, Total Quality Management and Six Sigma. Whilst all of these approaches have their advantages, the most important factor is to ensure that people are actively monitoring and measuring effectiveness and efficiency at all levels of the organisation, and feel empowered to question or suggest changes.

It is also crucial to ensure that any localised changes do not cause problems for other areas. For example, a sales team might find recording extensive client information rather laborious when making a sale – but this information may become crucial for the finance team when sending an invoice. End-to-end processes should be considered, and any knock-on impact should be assessed.

How

1. Involve a wide range of stakeholders – at all levels in the organisation – in problem-solving activity. Ensure their voices are heard, and ensure that they feel that they can raise issues and potential improvements too.

2. Implement suggestion schemes and openly welcome suggestions for potential improvements. Ensure each suggestion is replied to – even if a suggestion is not practical, people will appreciate a considered response.

3. Ensure that senior and middle managers are behind the idea and support continuous improvements. Ensure that everybody is underlining the importance of this when they speak to teams.

4. When implementing solutions to problems, make it clear that there is room for pivoting and tweaking, and ensure that the team feel empowered to make these suggestions.

5. Where appropriate, make the KPIs (success measures) of the problem-solving initiative public. Show how well the solution is

working. If there is a gap in performance, solicit suggestions on how to plug it. This should *never* be a blame exercise – it should be about pulling on the collective expertise to iron out any final creases and get the solution working as near to perfect as possible.

Reflection

- How did it work?

- What will I do next time?

References

ASQ, n.d. *Continuous Improvement.* Available at: http://asq.org/ learn-about-quality/continuous-improvement/overview/ overview.html

Conclusions and next steps

I hope that you have found this book interesting and useful. As we have discussed throughout this book, for our problem-solving activities to be successful, it is vital that we avoid falling into the trap of inadvertently adopting a knee-jerk solution. Thinking divergently, focussing on outcomes, and consciously structuring our problem solving will help avoid some of these traps.

Taking time to define a problem with a problem statement, define the desired outcomes (with CSFs and KPIs) and create a problem canvas will ensure that the problem-solving team and any relevant stakeholders are all on 'the same page' with regards to the problem that is being examined. This will save time in the long run, as it will enable us to avoid scurrying down dead ends that do not lead us anywhere useful.

Challenging ourselves – and our stakeholders – to think differently about problems will help us deliver appropriate solutions, and achieve the outcomes that our organisations need.

If you found this book useful, I'd encourage you to visit the book's companion website at www.problemsolvingbook.co.uk. You can download a copy of the problem canvas for free, and you can immediately start using this in your organisation. Other content will be added over the coming months too, so do take a regular look.

Finally, please *do* let me know how you get on. I would love to hear how your problem-solving initiatives are progressing and how you have used and adapted the techniques mentioned in this book.

Until next time,

Adrian Reed
Principal Consultant,
Blackmetric Business Solutions
adrian.reed@problemsolvingbook.co.uk

What did you think of this book?

We're really keen to hear from you about this book, so that we can make our publishing even better.

Please log on to the following website and leave us your feedback.

It will only take a few minutes and your thoughts are invaluable to us.

www.pearsoned.co.uk/bookfeedback

References and further reading

ASQ, n.d. *Continuous Improvement*. Available at: http://asq.org/
learn-about-quality/continuous-improvement/overview/
overview.html [accessed 25 October 2015].

Association for Project Management (APM), n.d. *What is Project
Management?* Available at: https://www.apm.org.uk/WhatIsPM
[accessed 16 November 2015].

Blackmetric Business Solutions. Further information at www.
blackmetric.co.uk

Cadle, J., Paul, D. and Turner, P., 2014. *Business Analysis Techniques:
99 Essential Tools for Success*. Swindon: BCS.

Davis, J.R. and Atkinson, T., 2010. 'Need speed? Slow down'. *Harvard
Business Review*, May.

International Institute of Business Analysis (IIBA), 2009. *A Guide to
the Business Analysis Body of Knowledge® (BABOK® Guide)*, v2.
Toronto: IIBA.

International Institute of Business Analysis (IIBA), 2015. *A Guide to
the Business Analysis Body of Knowledge® (BABOK® Guide)*, v3.
Toronto: IIBA.

Kahneman, D., 2012. *Thinking, Fast and Slow*. London: Penguin.

Kaplan, R.S. and Norton, D.P., 1996. *The Balanced Scorecard:
Translating Strategy Into Action*. Boston, MA: Harvard Business
School Press.

Kotter, J., 1996. *Leading Change*. Boston: Harvard Business Press.

Liker, J.K. and Convis, G.L., 2012. *The Toyota Way to Lean Leadership*.
US: McGraw-Hill.

National Audit Office, 2011. *The Failure of the FiReControl Project*.
London: NAO.

Oxford Dictionaries, n.d. *Oxford English Dictionary*. Available at:
http://www.oxforddictionaries.com/definition/english/holistic
[accessed 6 December 2015].

Paul, D., Cadle, J. and Yeates, D. (eds), 2014. *Business Analysis*. Third
Edition. Swindon: BCS.

References and further reading

Perspectiv, n.d. *Creative Problem Solving – The Swiss Army Knife for BAs*. London: Presented at BA Conference Europe 2011.

Podeswa, H., 2009. *The Business Analyst's Handbook*. Boston: Course Technology PTR, a part of Cengage Learning.

Pullan, P. and. Archer. J., 2013. *Business Analysis and Leadership*. London: Kogan Page.

Reed, A., n.d. *Adrian Reed's Blog*. Available at: www.adrianreed.co.uk

Ries, E., 2011. *The Lean Startup*. London: Portfolio Penguin.

Rumelt, R., 2011. *Good Strategy/Bad Strategy: The Difference and Why it Matters*. London: Profile Books.

Sirkin, H.L. and. Stalk, G., 1990. 'Fix the process, not the problem', *Harvard Business Review*, July–August.

Index

Index